Table of Contents

Introduction

The collection of essays compiled in this book is the conference proceedings from the first Cross-Atlantic Creativity Congress (CACC), which was held on April 4, 2022, in Salzburg, Austria. With participants ranging from international scholars, business executives, artists, cultural managers, educators, policymakers, and more, the purpose of the CACC was to spark interest in how creativity can be learned, studied, measured, and predicted regarding the future of innovation capabilities and society's resilience. As the first of its kind, this event strove to make creativity more tangible through widespread conversations and synergies about understanding and disseminating creativity from a scientific point of view.

We would like to thank our partners Innovation Salzburg GmbH / Interreg Crossinno, Salzburg Global Seminar, Paris Lodron Universität Salzburg, University of Colorado Denver's Imaginator Academy, Jake Jabs Center for Entrepreneurship at the University of Colorado Denver, City of Salzburg, Salzburg County, Startup Salzburg, Penn State University, MINT Labs, and Society for the Neuroscience of Creativity for their support.

Welcome Notes

Brigitta Pallauf, President of the Salzburg State Parliament

"In the beginning, God created heaven and earth." In discussing the topic of creativity, it would be prudent to start at the very beginning, before Adam and Eve. The term 'creativity' dates back to God's creation of the world from nothing. He was inspired by freedom, both in artistic production and in political action. Freedom and joy form a combination in the context of creativity and creative power. For creative people, motivation comes from within. Their actions stem from desire and joy. They love the tension between chaos and order, fantasy and reality.

With that in mind, we can breathe a sigh of relief and jump to the 18th century, when a man named Friedrich Schiller shed some interesting insight. Freedom and joy can be found in the game. Schiller said, "Man only plays where he is human in the full meaning of the word, and he is only fully human where he plays" (1797). Of course, he was not referring to card games or dice, but he was rather concerned with a change in society for the better. That's another keyword, after freedom and joy, because creativity is all about the future.

This leads us to examine C.G. Jung in the 20th century. Man has a natural need for development and Jung speaks of the process of individuation. He wanted to contribute to something bigger. Creativity and interdisciplinary encounters are part of it. Unlike God, however, the creative human being does not draw on nothing. The knowledge of the world forms a framework. Creativity, it seems, dispenses with planning and therefore poses a potential danger of 'counter-creativity' if the imperative "Be creative!" is too strong. Creative thinking also works differently than problem-solving - it asks questions for which there are no problems yet and therefore disturbs people.

In the here and now, specifically at the Cross-Atlantic Congress for Creativity, we are trying to make this wonderful human quality fruitful for our future, especially in this time of crisis. Salzburg is a city that has intensively and sustainably developed a science and innovation strategy up to 2025 and is taking powerful steps towards its achievement. Wolfgang Amadeus Mozart impressively demonstrates the fact that creativity can be great even under problematic circumstances. However, as many know, he did not love Salzburg. "You know, best friend, how I hate Salzburg! Salzburg is not a place for my talent," he once said. Despite that, he did compose one of his most wonderful works here, the Coronation Mass, first heard 243 years ago in the Salzburg Cathedral.

We are proud and grateful to welcome you here to the CACC, in the heart of Europe. Unlike Mozart, we aim to prove impressively that this heart also beats for an international competence for creativity.

Thank You!

1. Why Walk If You Can Fly Using Your Creativity?

Seda Röder, Founder of The Sonophilia Foundation

Ponder this: Why are you here? What's the meaning of life? Perhaps I can answer that question, but let's take a more scientific detour first. Just to make things less obscure, we can start by asking: What is the purpose of having a brain?

The question sounds like a joke, right? You will be surprised, but it is indeed a legitimate scientific question, as several species have no brains (like sea stars or oysters), but they are still capable of living.

For the most part, neuroscientists agree that we need a brain to move. The sea squirt, despite its humorous name, offers some proof of this notion: this little animal has a brain, moves forward, and searches for the perfect place to settle. Once it finds it, it eats its own brain. The search is complete, rendering its brain unnecessary. We humans, on the other hand, luckily don't tend to eat our brains, probably because we are always searching for a better place. We're all inherently curious and creative! It stands to reason, then, that our brains are also made to move. However, we also want to be moved!

Unfortunately, it seems that some of us have given up on the "search" or are being pushed into a sea squirt-like existence. However, do we have the luxury of wasting all those brains and all that potential? Global warming, drastic changes in the labor market, the dawn of AI, exponential technologies, fake news, pandemics, and social inequality - these are just some of the big problems awaiting innovative solutions that will benefit everyone.

But where do innovations come from?

They certainly don't appear out of thin air. Behind all innovations is a person or a group of people who were able to search, imagine, and build a better future.

We've hit a snag, though. Outsourcing the search to a handful of people we call the "experts" has become the norm. The number of issues that need our attention far outnumbers the experts exploring them. For example, according to Statistik Austria, there are approximately 10 million experts – scientists, engineers or otherwise qualified people – working in innovation, research & development related to medicine, pharmaceuticals, social sciences, technology, mobility, new materials, service innovation, or environment. There are approximately 7 billion living on earth. The aforementioned 10 million, which happens to be less than 0.1% of the global population (!), are thus holding our future in their hands. What an unsettling correlation!

Let's shift to a business perspective. A research group led by Vijay Govindajaran of Dartmouth University found that in a typical company, at least 5% of people seem to be born innovators. That 5% would make great intrapreneurs; their creativity could bring tremendous value to the business. However, most companies are unable to actually execute on this kind of potential.

The learning?

We obviously have enough people to solve our many problems, but what we lack is a better way to leverage and integrate their creative power. We have prejudices and rigid systems that allow only certain kinds of people to contribute to the innovative process. We forget that creativity is an inherent potential, that it can be learned, and that it can come from every corner of life. If we allowed creativity to flourish and permeate our lives, we could have many more people contributing to the solutions to all problems, big or small, personal or collective. The only way to accelerate solutions is by scaling up the creative potential, and that's only possible if we find a better way to distribute creative power.

Let me give you an example: Guadalupe Cruz, was eight years old, coming from Chiapas, one of the poorest states in Mexico, when she constructed a solar-powered device made out of trash to heat water for families in her community. In 2018, she was the first child ever to win the Nuclear Science Award at the National University of Mexico and was recognized as an outstanding young innovator by Time magazine.

Creative potential is everywhere, but only some are as lucky as Guadalupe to have their solutions recognized and shared with those most in need.

Another example is Mr. Thomas Royen, 76 years old and retired for over 10 years. Eight years ago, he solved one of the biggest problems in math: the Gaussian correlation inequality. He then tried to get his solution recognized by the right people and published in peer-reviewed journals. However, he couldn't succeed because no one knew who he was. The experts continued to work on that same problem for two more years until two young Polish mathematicians coincidentally discovered and promoted his solution!

These and similar cases are precisely why we founded the Sonophilia Foundation: our non-profit organization exists to help everybody's creativity flourish and to bring those undiscovered innovations to light. Our purpose is to democratize creativity and to make creativity a tangible science that is approachable to everyone.

Talking about creativity is a difficult task despite its being rather ubiquitous; it's still lofty and elusive. Nevertheless, the World Economic Forum states creativity is one of the top five skills needed to thrive in the future. An IBM CEO study from as early as 2010 similarly says that creativity will be the single most important quality for a CEO, even more important than managerial skills. But, what does that even mean?

Talking about creativity today is like talking about God in the Middle Ages. Everything we can't grasp or explain about excellence and achievement is attributed to creativity.

We at the Sonophilia Foundation see creativity more like electricity in the Enlightenment. We know this phenomenon occurs, but we lack the wire, the kite and the key to make it visible. This is changing. We're finally entering the Ben Franklin era of creativity – as the Sonophilian Andy Zmolek once put it. Many of the myths about divine inspirations, overnight eureka moments or genetic predispositions are one by one, being debunked by scientific research studies. We end up with a pretty clear picture of the importance of nurture.

With the advancements in instruments and the dawn of neuroimaging technologies, we can now look at the brain during creative activities. We can see that neurons make connections with each other and the more often a connection is repeated, the more it is fortified. Creativity looks magical, but it's not magic. It is a very natural process taking place in our bodies, which are perfectly prewired for this kind of work. We're not even using a fraction of what we're capable of achieving.

To give this concept some context, Hannah Merseal previously received Sonophilia Foundation's Outstanding Young Scientist Award in Creativity Research, which aims to look deeper into what happens during creative activities, such as associative thinking, ideation, mind-wandering, or improvisation. She's also involved with creativity measurement and our upcoming creativity factbook project.

We need to get the scientific facts out into the world! Talking about eureka tales or overnight bursts of divine inspiration makes creative achievements look as if they happen spontaneously: Since we typically only witness the moment of hatching, we often forget the importance of the incubation period. The nurture and care aspects are just as essential, if not more so; they help ensure that everyone can develop their creative confidence.

Research shows that we share 98% of our genetic makeup with chimpanzees, but what makes us different is our ingenuity. Everything interesting, important, intriguing, moving, and thus human, arises from our creativity. It is what gives our lives meaning and fulfills our brains' purpose.

In a nutshell, this is why we founded the Sonophilia Foundation. We have two major large-scale projects and initiatives:

1. At the Sonophilia Institute of Applied Creativity, together with our scientific partners at PennState University and the Society for the Neuroscience of

Creativity, we want to understand how creativity works in the brain and how we can help more people benefit from the insights provided by the scientific research of creativity. The idea is to optimize and update human education and business and make way for more creativity in all facets of life. Creativity is still the one thing that gives our species a competitive advantage over computers!

2. Matters.Global is an ambitious initiative that centers around a global collaboration platform to define and frame problems as explained by the people who experience them. You can think of this like Wikipedia, not for answers but for questions. What are all the problems we need to solve and how are those problems related? It resembles a mindmap of problems. We collect thousands of problems and then analyze their similarities and differences. Once we find big clusters of problems and their interrelatedness, we can then concentrate our resources first on those that have the maximum impact. At matters.global, everybody's creativity is relevant and people can contribute to finding or linking problems by playing a simple game we created, called My 99 Problems!

If creating the world's biggest virtual map of problems or making creativity a tangible science gives you goosebumps, join our pursuit at www.sonophiliafoundation.org

I believe the meaning of life is to create meaning. We are all here to move and be moved, but indeed the question remains: Why walk if you can fly using your creativity?

2. Creativity In The Fields Of Mathematics, Statistics, And Data Science.

Arne C. Bathke, Professor of Statistics and Dean of the Digital & Analytical Sciences at Salzburg University

Perhaps a small disclaimer is justified before delving into the topic of creativity: I have not done any explicit research into creativity, so all my musings are based on my experience as a human being who has most likely been using creativity without much thinking about it, just as many of us. I wouldn't claim to know how creativity "works". However, as I have been invited to speak specifically as a mathematician/statistician/data scientist, I can say a little bit about the creative process in these closely interconnected fields.

Let me structure this short essay by first considering creativity in mathematics, and then in statistics and data science. Within these disciplines, creative elements exist in each step of the scientific process - summarized in the following short and likely non-exhaustive list:

1. Discovering (or inventing) results.
2. Proving or justifying the findings.
3. Applying the results in the real world.
4. Communicating mathematical (statistical, data science) content.

Starting with the field of mathematics and step (1), one of the fundamental questions is whether we create and invent ("erfinden" in German) new things, or whether everything in mathematics basically already exists and we just discover ("finden") it. Similar questions may be asked in other abstract or structural disciplines, or even in fields such as arts and music. However, the question about inventing vs. discovering doesn't seem to apply straightforwardly to disciplines such as the material sciences, engineering, or technology, where an essential part of an invention is a smart combination of (often tangible) things that have been invented before. Think of cars or smartphones, for example. In such a context, most people would argue that the creative process involves rearranging several existing human-made products while using the associated knowledge.

On the other hand, one may argue that the famous numbers that appear to be holding the world together (0, 1, pi, e, sqrt(-1), and so forth) were already in principle out there before someone discovered their beautiful properties and came up with ways to formalize working with them. The same applies to the natural constants known in physics, as well as to the mathematical theorems, from simple to complex. Once a few basic axioms are set, all the results that can be derived from these axioms do already exist in some sense, long before the first person has proved them. One may even suggest that creation or creativity in mathematics somewhat resembles the biblical idea of creation as "making something out of nothing". The mathematical structures that one may define and then evaluate can be considered pure and abstract and made out of nothing, even if they are often motivated by reality. Are they inventions, or are they discoveries? We'll have to leave the answer to this question open. I would even argue that there is no right or wrong answer, but that thinking about it may nevertheless still be enlightening or interesting.

Let us come to the more practical questions. Assuming that mathematical facts are "found", how do we go about finding them? How does a mathematical result such as the Central Limit Theorem (showing that the Gaussian or normal distribution is a good approximation for many processes) appear on the radar of mathematicians as something that could hold true? Why should it hold? In general, how do we find results which we think could be true?

Here, mathematics is very similar to pretty much every other discipline. To create something, you need to be familiar with the language and the tools of the discipline. You never create "out of nothing", but you rather use all the tools available to you in the discipline. A broad knowledge of mathematical facts, methods and their possible interrelations does help in the creative process. In addition to the toolbox arising from within the field, inspiration may also come from the real world around us. The field of mathematics in general - indeed many specific mathematical methods and models - has been invented to provide a precise and efficient description of the world around us. Furthermore, ideas for statements that may be formulated as mathematical facts may come from other scientific disciplines that describe the world around us and in us, from physics to biology and medicine, from the geosciences to the life sciences. Finally, the discipline of mathematics has grown so much that different subfields may seem far apart, but they still provide mutual inspiration and ideas through similarities and analogies; they are connected by a common basic language that reflects a structured way towards formalizing statements and making them precise.

All of this is part of the creative process: Seeing analogies that are not obvious at first sight, and seeing how different individual things (facts, methods, processes) that are drawn from within mathematics, from the other sciences, or the real world around us, can be connected or combined, although they appear to be rather unrelated at first sight. Thus, also in the mathematical sciences, many (or most) scientific discoveries are combinations, extensions, or generalizations of findings that were already available at the outset of a specific research project. In that sense, research is almost always incremental; this holds true for mathematics, just as for most other scientific disciplines.

As the house of mathematics has become rather vast and complex, nowadays a mathematician may live their scientific life completely inside this house, without the need for inspiration from the real world, or other scientific fields. We call this "pure mathematics", namely mathematics for the sake of itself. On the other hand, typical "applied mathematicians" actively seek out collaborative projects with scientists from other disciplines, draw inspiration from real-world problems, or see their mathematical findings applied in practice. Both flavors of mathematics can be highly rewarding: Carl Friedrich Gauß stated that there could be no greater joy and satisfaction to the thinking mind than working on the solution to the intellectually most challenging problems. In my personal view, however, it can be even more rewarding to see formal findings "at work" in a completely different discipline or solve real-life challenges affecting humankind.

In any case, as all mathematicians share the beautiful and efficient formal language of mathematics, many findings from fundamental "pure math" are eventually "translated", often by applied mathematicians, and thus they do find their way into applied work - just as findings from fundamental research in other disciplines are being translated into the real world.

Now to step (2). How about mathematically proving something we think could be true?

Proving a mathematical statement essentially means convincing other people with a sufficient degree of mathematical knowledge that the statement must be true. There are general strategies for mathematical proofs that every student learns in their first year.

However, as one might imagine, it depends on the person you are trying to convince of a statement's truth how much detail you will need to provide in a proof. Experts could be satisfied with a general idea and outline, as they may immediately see whether a proof will be valid, while mathematical novices need to be presented with a very detailed proof that is clearly structured and can be understood line by line.

In addition to strategy and level of detail, the third dimension of a proof is the type of mathematical language being used. To non-mathematicians, it may sound strange at first, but the language of mathematics has evolved quite a bit. It has become more precise and efficient over the centuries - and this trend is still ongoing. Some statements that we now formulate as one-liners using modern mathematical language would have taken a page or more, with many more words and fewer mathematical symbols, 200 years ago, and would have been quasi-impossible to formulate even earlier. There are many parallels to the familiar spoken languages. The language of mathematics is a living language that is constantly being developed further to satisfy a need for more precise and efficient communication, but the language in turn also affects how mathematical research and instruction are being conducted. It affects the creative process that uses this mathematical language. Indeed, sometimes the key to a mathematical discovery or a proof is using the right language to formulate and structure a problem. The use of (mathematical) language can therefore be integral to the creative process.

The points just described for mathematics also hold in large part for statistics, data science, artificial intelligence, and related fields. If you want to formulate relevant facts in a very precise manner in any of these fields, you need to use the language of mathematics, and we have already seen that this is a language that keeps developing. Compared to mathematics, research in these latter fields generally has a closer connection to the real world and other disciplines, to draw inspiration and to apply new findings, and in these fields, there are, in part, other toolkits available to obtain ideas regarding which statements could be true and provable, and also for verifying (or falsifying) them. In statistics, for example, it has become a common practice since the 1970s to supplement theoretical research findings with computer simulations, and computer simulations are also utilized to identify potential findings or to fine-tune them. In the last two decades, newly published research in statistics and data science is often accompanied by open-source software. This not only allows other statisticians to reproduce findings and simulation results but also facilitates the use of said methods by researchers in other fields whose feedback may subsequently spark new research directions.

Drawing on experience appears to be a central component of creativity, but experience is also a key to becoming a good statistician or data scientist because research findings in these fields almost inevitably need to be set into a context of reality and evaluated in that regard. This is even considered a point of distinction between statistics and mathematics, as one could technically be a successful mathematician without much life experience. It has been said that the field of mathematics resembles music, while statistics resemble literature: There are child prodigies in the former, but not in the latter, as the former requires talent and training, while the latter also requires life experience (De Vaux and Velleman (2008): Math is Music; Statistics is Literature – or Why are there no six-year-old Novelists?).

The accumulated experience is also instrumental in step (4), namely communicating the findings. Statisticians and data scientists often have to explain the conclusions from their analyses to laypeople (here: people who are untrained in the statistical sciences), much more than scientists in most other fields. Thus, findings have to be simplified without distorting them, while keeping the essential elements understandable and interpretable. Indeed, professional statisticians often devote a significant portion of time that has been allotted to a research project ensuring that the findings can be interpreted correctly. Also, the European Statistics Code of Practice specifically states that "Statistics [...] are presented [...] in a form that facilitates proper interpretation and meaningful comparisons."

Most statisticians spend the first years of their academic careers talking about models, methods, and data with other statisticians until at some point, they have to explain findings to non-statisticians for the first time. They then find out how much more challenging this is, and how much spontaneous creativity it requires. If they survive this experience and succeed, they also discover how rewarding these interdisciplinary interactions can be.

While these lines could only cover selected aspects of the mathematical and statistical sciences, I hope that they have shed a bit of light on how creativity comes into play during the central steps of research in these fields and on some parallels and differences between these and other disciplines. In statistics, much of the creative process is inspired by interdisciplinary interactions. Therefore, I close with a poem that is dedicated to interdisciplinarity.

Interdisciplinarity.

- It means no hiding behind your fancy lingo.
- You become vulnerable because about most areas of research – you don't know much.
- You and your science may be challenged fundamentally.
- You are representing a whole field. Scary.
- But you can give something from your knowledge.
- You may make a contribution within a team of top experts (in other fields).
- You can dare to tackle big issues, together—team spirit.
- You're having fun. Great fun. If you're lucky, you can almost feel how creativity is at work.
- You may inspire others.

3. Spot On MozART: Visualizing Music In The Digital Age.

Thomas Ballhausen, Magdalena Karner, Franziska Wallner, Mozarteum University

"Music, which comes from the muses, cannot be considered one among the arts. It is the sum of all the arts. No art can be successful if it has no music."

- **Michel Serres**

Asking Relevant Questions

What do you see when you listen to Mozart? This is the key question we ask ourselves every day in the Spot On MozART project. In a strongly image-oriented society, it is of the utmost importance to not just surrender to the omnipresent worlds of images, but rather to actively shape them. The power of images lies not only in our helplessness before them, but in the call to create images of the present and, for us in particular, to take up the possibilities of technological innovation and digital tools to do that within an art-driven project.

To focus more heavily on the vital connection between acoustic and visual perception, research is being conducted at the university level on various approaches to the production, distribution and reception of audiovisuality. Spot On MozART, which is set to run through the year 2023, is an internationally successful example of this endeavour, based at the University Mozarteum Salzburg. Spot on MozART is an inter-university and interdisciplinary project that aims to provide a visual exploration of listening and thus a new understanding and visualization of Mozart and his work. At the intersection between art, science and technology, students and teachers from international universities, as well as renowned partners from culture, business and technology, are developing visualizations of selected works by Mozart. Under the umbrella of Spot On MozART, up to 50 so-called work projects, ranging from music videos to short feature films, from media installations to digital apps, will have been created between 2020 and 2023.

Providing A Lean Framework

In our experience, when almost everything is allowed in a project, relatively little works. Therefore, within Spot On MozART we decided to work with constructive constraints to foster activities and development. To support, document and evaluate the processes of the respective work projects as efficiently as possible, we have developed a portfolio document. This document contains the central fields of activity that each of the work projects must fulfill, starting from Mozart's music. Additionally, we consider the choice of a specific visualization, the use of innovative technologies, the form of public presentation as a so-called Spot On-moment, and the research aspect of the respective work project. In the interplay of these binding parts, the purpose of the project becomes more tangible and the production, distribution and reception are continuously reflected upon.

The governance structure of the Spot On MozART projects consists of the 'Office Team', the quality-controlling 'Steering Board', the 'Cluster Board' and the 'Advisory Board'. The office team are involved in all projects and guides them through all stages of development, production and publication. The five fields of activity defined in the portfolio are binding for all work projects, while all other aspects are adapted accordingly. We have worked successfully with very different, international institutions and companies, including TU Vienna, Moonlake Entertainment, IXA, and Creative Robotics. In Spot On MozART, large and small partners stand side by side on an equal footing - universities next to research institutions, and international corporations next to regional companies. We prioritize collaboration over competition, which is sometimes harder than it sounds. We focus on solutions, build coalitions, and keep the slush moving, so to speak. In Spot On MozART, we create a sense of belonging to foster creative work and real cooperation. We translated our purpose into a plan and laid out specific structures to connect the respective players under pre-defined rules. Our job is also to maintain this dynamic choreography, to

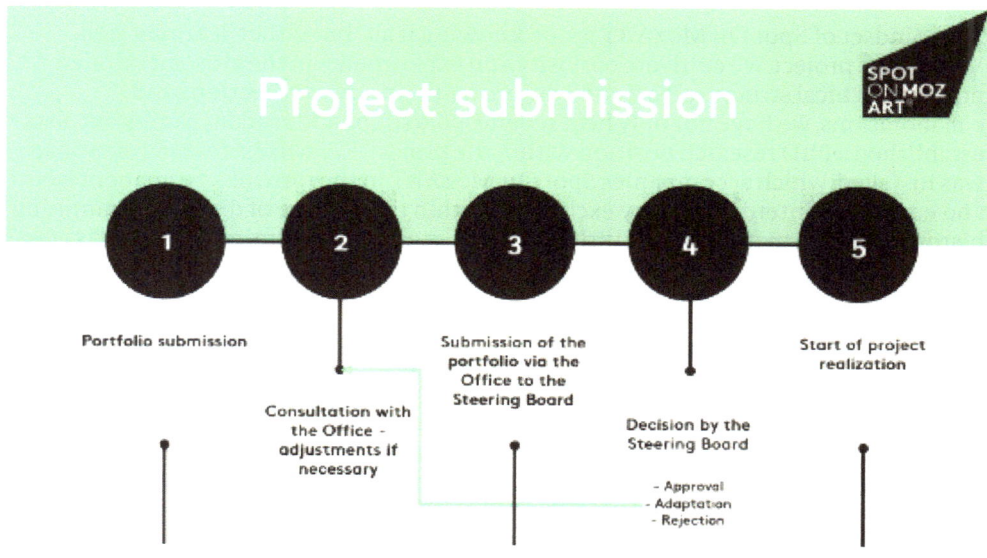

keep being agile and flexible, and to not mistake the complex for the complicated.

Combining Cultural Heritage And Innovative Technology.

With Spot On MozART, we have not only articulated a clear purpose but have also secured the necessary resources to experiment and test. We have established a well-balanced process to deliver real results. Spot On MozART is proactive in bringing together cultural heritage and technological innovation in a sound economic framework. The fact that the project is a success story for 'Culture Tech' is also because, for us, cultural heritage is not only material for the worst-case stress test of technological developments, but we deliberately rely on the intertwining of culture and technology. Our art-driven approach is based on an understanding of narrative, innovation and how technological means can help create and distribute culture in all its forms and expressions.

We, therefore, think of Austrian cultural heritage in a European context and from a global perspective. We open up artistic and critical perspectives on a work that can be reacquainted. For the Spot On MozART team, it is clear that we have irrevocably arrived in the Digital Age. All aspects of our lives are permeated by technology, including the manifold connections between the arts, business, and technological innovation. Mozarteum is the only art university with a music-driven project that won a highly competitive grant within the scope of the federal initiative for digital and social transformation – which has reaffirmed the validity of our thinking and approach. We can only thrive in a changed and ever-changing world if we ensure real cooperation, real-world results and applications, and preserve our cultural heritage.

The mindset of Spot On MozART is not 'knowing it all,' but rather 'learning it all.' Within the project, we cultivate curiosity and experiments in the aforementioned non-hierarchical structure. To establish and maintain new connections and collaborations, we have not only held several workshops and student camps but also established a PhD research position within the project. Likewise, a research seminar was installed, which accompanies Spot On MozART in the form of a permanent lab and enables an interdisciplinary exchange. Within this culture of dialogue, examining historical source material or acquiring new skill sets, such as filming or coding, is supplemented by a constant exchange with national partners. These include Research Studios Austria (RSA FG) or international partners such as the Royal College of Music London.

Fostering Real Impact And Results.

Spot On MozART has had an innovative and positive effect on several relevant areas. For example, it has helped facilitate the exemplary implementation of new course formats for the framework of our university. An interdisciplinary research seminar accompanies ongoing student-centered research and development projects and conveys the main contents of scientific theoretical models and methods. In a workshop format developed in spring 2022, which will be applied from the current summer semester onwards, new forms of artistic research can be tested together with the Red Bull media archive and put into effect in the form of artistic projects. Positive impulses, which can also be seen in the permanent intra-university dissemination activities, can thus be described as an expanded or entirely new interdisciplinary cooperation. These are demonstrated in the development of new master's programmes in scenography and the design of internal university funding projects.

Moreover, Spot On MozART acts as a best practice example for current national and international submissions, both in its overall structure and in the form of work projects that have already been successfully executed. For the impact within the framework of the project's partner universities, we must highlight not only the general establishment or strengthening of professional exchange but also the reinforcement of cooperation with the cross-university science and art cluster, new collaborations with regional partners, as well as the music-oriented collaboration with selected partners. For the corresponding effects within the framework of the project cluster, we see the interaction between education, research and business to be particularly enhanced. Based on our work projects, independent spin-off initiatives have emerged and continue to crop up, which shows how effective art and music education can prove. Within the Austrian university system, we cite the practice-oriented expansion of competencies for audio-visuality, artistic research and cultural/critical heritage, which is guided, facilitated and continuously advanced by Spot On MozART. As a unique national and international art-driven lighthouse project, Spot On MozART

Five fields of activity

SPOT ON MOZ ART

The scientific treatment of a research question.
RESEARCH

The placement in space and society.
SPOT ON

MUSIC
Starting point and immanent factor at all fields of activity.

VISUALISATION
A digital, artistic, visually designed interpretation of Mozart's music.

INNOVATION
The project and production immanent factor that runs through all fields of action.

proves to be a positive example of results-centered work in the field of culture tech.

Next Steps.

The visualizations of Spot On MozART currently range from short feature films to virtual reality environments, from music videos to mobile phone applications, and from documentaries to media installations. As diverse and multifaceted as our partners are in the respective work projects, so too are the results. The current projects also focus on the aforementioned fields of activity around Mozart's music, as well as on the permanent internationalization and expansion of the media formats used. The network of Spot On MozART is constantly growing and we still have more than a year to develop and implement new projects. When working with new partners, it remains essential for us to combine our general purpose with all strategic decisions. We set our expectations with realistic optimism, but strive to bridge the gaps between the different communities we work with. We see our task as a rewarding one aimed at bringing forward a different future of learning, researching and developing. Realistically, this means creating a microcosm of the world we want, one which we won't give up on.

*Literature for this article can be found on Pages 87-88

4. Creative Thinking: Spontaneous Or Strategic?

Dr. Roger Beaty, Director of the Cognitive Neuroscience of Creativity Lab at PennState University

I want to talk about some of the research I've been doing on the neuroscience of creativity. To be a little bit more specific, I'll be talking about creative thinking. I'll start with some of the big questions that have motivated my research over the years.

Perhaps one of the biggest questions is: How does the brain produce creative thought? Where do creative ideas come from? How does the brain flexibly piece together information to help us solve problems with no obvious solution? Is creative thinking spontaneous or strategic? By that, I mean, do creative ideas pop into our minds out of nowhere, or is there a deliberate process that exerts some level of control in our brains? Finally, is the creative brain wired differently, meaning is there some pattern of neural wiring in the brain that differentiates someone more creative from someone who is less creative?

Many people are probably familiar with the definition of creativity and creative thinking in psychology and neuroscience literature, which states that it is the ability to produce something novel and useful. It's not usually enough just to come up with something that hasn't existed before; it should solve some problem or be effective. I'll be talking about divergent thinking, a specific kind of creative thinking that involves generating multiple possible ideas that diverge from a certain topic or concept. The nice thing about the tests that are used to measure divergent thinking is they tend to correlate with real-world creative hobbies and achievements. People who tend to do well on these tests tend to do creative things in their everyday lives, so, we would say they have some level of validity.

To unpack divergent thinking a little more, it is the ability to generate divergent ideas as they move away from a given starting point. They're often measured with either verbal, psychological tests or drawing-based tests. People are shown an initial starting point, which could be some scribbles on the page, and they have to imagine some way to complete this figure. I think the verbal-based side helps to distinguish divergent thinking from what's called convergent thinking. With convergent thinking, you're trying to converge on a correct answer or a single optimal solution. Think of an intelligence test, for example. There's only one right answer. Usually, with divergent thinking, you're moving away, and there are many possible solutions. There's no right answer.

I'll demonstrate this with some examples. The remote associates test is a classic convergent thinking problem where people are presented with three words, and they have to think of a fourth word that is related to all three. These kinds of problems can be answered or solved through insight, where the solution just pops into your mind spontaneously or more analytically as you're working through the possible answers. I think this is a very interesting type of creative thinking.

I'd like to focus more on divergent thinking. I think people have heard of this or have come across these alternate uses tests before, where you're presented with different objects and you have to think of creative ways to use the objects (e.g., a brick). Normally, when people are trying to think of ideas, they will say things like "use it to build a house." However, sometimes people will say, "use it as a doorstop," which is moving a little bit further away. Some people have said "using it as an exfoliator." This may be on the novel side and less on the useful or less painful side. Perhaps someone might say "to grind it up and make a filtering substance," which is a more clever answer. You can see there's a wide range of the kinds of ideas people come up with. This is just one way you can use to understand the general ability of people to come up with different ideas that are often used in the scientific study of creativity.

Next, I want to walk through a couple of the theories that have been proposed over the years to try to explain how creative thinking works. One of the theories is called the associative theory. According to this theory, creative thinking involves spontaneously connecting concepts in memory, or semantic memory, which is our collective database of facts and concepts that we've acquired throughout our lives.

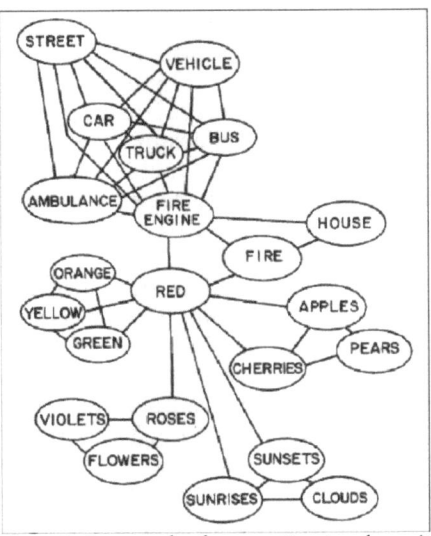

Figure 1: An example of a semantic network map[iv]

[1]Collins, A. M., & Loftus, E. F. (1975). A spreading-activation theory of semantic processing. Psychological Review,

Above is a toy example of a semantic network where we have concepts that are closely related conceptually. We have colors clustering together, along with different fruits. Of course, this exact thing does not exist in our brains, but this is thought to be an abstract representation of the concepts that we've acquired over time. If you want to think creatively, you want to make connections between things that are far apart. This is one way that people might be differing in their creative abilities: the way that they organize these concepts in memory. If you are trying to make a connection between things that are otherwise pretty dissimilar, or if you're representing that closer in your memory, it might be easier to make those kinds of connections. This is just one theory on how creative thinking might work, especially when it comes to connecting concepts.

Another theory has been termed executive theory. This emphasizes more controlled aspects of thinking or executive functions, such as inhibition, controlling attention, monitoring, and working memory. The main idea is that you're trying to exert some level of control over your thinking; you're focusing your attention and working hard on a problem. Things may be getting spontaneously connected in a more undirected way.

Executive functions generally help us to manage the contents of our minds, thoughts, emotions, and behaviors. The reason why this might be beneficial for creative thinking is often that we're trying to move away from what we already know. We have to get past the obvious ideas and redirect our thinking to more fruitful lines of thought.

With these two contrasting theories, I've been trying for some time to bring them together to acknowledge that it's not just one or the other, but maybe it can be both. I and others have been working on what's called dual process theories. This is the idea that we have both associative and spontaneous thinking, as well as more strategic and directed types of thinking. We've done studies showing that both of them are predictors of people's ability to think divergently. If you're familiar with system one and system two kinds of thinking, this is a combination of both. One question I've been interested in for a long time now is how these two things work in our brains, especially at the same time when we have spontaneous thinking and controlled thinking. How do we reconcile them? How do we harness both of them to help us to think creatively?

I'm going to walk through a model that I've been developing for several years now, which focuses on brain networks. When we talk about networks, we're talking about many different things that are connected and working together and exchanging information. If you've ever seen an fMRI study of brain activation of blobs of color on the brain, it's not that it's the connections between the blobs that are of interest here. One of the networks that we have in our brains that has been associated with creative thinking is called the default network, or the default mode network. It is referred to this because if you're in a brain scanner, and you're in a relaxed state, you're not being asked to do anything, so this network will pop online, and it's associated with things like mind wandering, daydreaming, spontaneous thinking, thinking about a past experience, or imagining a possible experience. In other words, we're going inward and thinking to ourselves in a less directed kind of way. In general, if you think about what this network might be doing in terms of creative functions, it could be things like brainstorming, idea generation, or simulating possibilities.

We then have another network called the executive control network. This network supports those more directed aspects of thinking--more strategic thinking that requires focused attention. If you think about what this might mean for creative functions, it could be things like evaluating ideas. Perhaps you've come up with something and you want to see if it's going to work. You're thinking through it more deliberately and inhibiting the common ideas that can come to mind when you need to think beyond what you already know.

There's a third network called the salience network, which got its name because it's involved in picking up salient information in the environment, as well as internally. It plays a general role in switching between a more default mind-wandering state and a more controlled type of state. In terms of possible creative functions, the salience network might pick up on promising things in the environment or our internal worlds, and may be shifting between a more spontaneous generative and a more controlled and strategic evaluative mode of thinking. This is the general framework that I've been trying to develop, and we've been testing it over the years.

Before I get into some of the evidence in support of this, I'd like to take a step back and point out that these networks seem to be doing different things. There's the one network that's involved in mind wandering, internally directed type thinking, where we're in our heads and the other network that's more controlled and focused. If you look at the neuroscience literature, there's been a longstanding finding that these networks don't work together, which makes sense, because they do different things. In one, when we're mind-wandering, we don't need to be focusing our attention; when we're focusing our attention, we don't need to be mind-wandering, which can be distracting. But if you look at the FMRI neuroscience literature, you can sometimes see one of the activation blobs or regions doing something and sometimes the other one's doing something. I have been fascinated by this. How might they work together? Is there some kind of communication between these two seemingly opposing ways of thinking?

We did a study on this with Mathias Benedec and others. We put people in an MRI scanner and asked them to think of creative uses for objects. We scanned their brains and looked for the communication patterns of the brain regions that were activated. Without unpacking all of the blobs on the screen, I will just say that we focused on a region that is within this default mode network, as well as other areas when people were thinking creatively. Sure enough, we found that it was communicating with the frontal parts of the brain that are more involved in those controlled aspects of thinking. So, you have this region that's more along the lines of spontaneous thinking.

Then you have the controlled areas that communicate with each other. We found that this pattern changed over time. When people were first starting to think of ideas, they were activating their default network; the salience network may have been picking up on the ideas, perhaps early on, and then later, when they were thinking of their ideas, more of the frontal areas were connected to this default area. This suggests that at the beginning when people were first thinking of ideas, they were using their default network. The salience network picks up on something promising and passes it along to the frontal parts of the brain that then evaluate whether it's any good or it's going to work.

Shortly after we published this paper, some studies came out that showed that similar patterns were found in the brains of performing musicians. There are these really fun studies where you put musicians in a brain scanner--an MRI scanner with an MRI-compatible keyboard that has no metal because MRI scanners are giant magnets, so you have to make some changes to make this work. We're also finding this same pattern in improvising musicians, as well as visual artists who are generating ideas for a book cover, and then evaluating how effective they were at meeting their goals. I'll try to interpret this in the framework I've been talking about so far, in the context of these studies.

With music improvisation, this is classically thought of as the most spontaneous type of creativity that exists; musicians are just coming up with new music on the spot and they don't have time to rehearse, but in this study, they were specifically asked to make their performances sound like something. They were given emotional cues and asked to improvise based on the idea of joy or sadness. The more controlled aspects of the brain might be communicating with this more spontaneous default network because it's constraining in a sense, how performance should look like. Instead of just coming up with anything at all, you want your performance to sound like something, so you're going to keep this idea in your mind as you're otherwise spontaneously coming up with new music. The way we interpreted this in a review paper, putting all these studies together, is by looking at the degree to which these networks might be communicating, specifically at whether it might have something to do with the constraints on thinking. It's not just "come up with whatever comes to your mind." It's rather "keep the guardrails on to some extent" and maintain a goal in your mind that continues to guide your performance.

To rewind to the slide where I showed you people in the scanner, doing the divergent thinking tasks. In an exploratory analysis where we looked at people that were less creative in the study, and those that were more creative in terms of their performance on this task, we found that they had more efficient wiring between those aforementioned networks. They exchanged information between these systems more efficiently. This raised the question, in my mind at the time, about whether there was some kind of individual difference between people that could explain why some people are much better at coming up with ideas than others.
We conducted a much larger study, and this was in collaboration with Yoed Kenett,

Mathis Benedek, and several others in the Proceedings of the National Academy of Sciences a few years ago. We used a machine-learning-based approach, in which we scanned almost 200 people doing divergent thinking. Out of the 35,000 possible connections that could have been uncovered with this approach, we found that the most relevant connections were within those three networks that I've been talking about so far: default, salience, and executive. Therefore, using this machine learning approach, we could predict how creative someone was on this task just by knowing the strength of the connections between these regions and networks. Sure enough, it extended to independent samples of people that weren't in our original study, so we built the model on almost 200 people. Then we tested it on a couple of other datasets. We found a consistent pattern that those who had stronger connections between these networks came up with better ideas.

Let's finally revisit the questions I posed at the beginning: is creative thinking spontaneous or strategic? It seems to be both - a classic answer in science. It's not one thing or another. It's almost always both. I'm interested in understanding how and when it's both. Sometimes it leans more towards one or the other, but these three networks that I've been talking about seem to work together in different ways to help people think creatively. In terms of why some people are more creative than others, at least on the divergence tasks I've been talking about, it seems to have something to do with their ability to bring together brain networks that typically do not work at the same time.

5. Elements Of Creative Cognition.

Mathias Benedek, Director of the Creative Cognition Lab at the University of Graz

Over the last several years, I have traveled a lot to attend creativity conferences around the world, but this is the first devoted international creativity conference taking place in Austria. It is a strong sign that the topic matters. I have researched creativity for over 15 years, and what has consistently puzzled me is how little we know about a construct that matters so much. Much has been done, yet there is much left to do. I want to share some insights from my work.

In many ways, creativity is a fascinating construct. On the one hand, creativity is very special. Creative ideas constantly shape our world, from minor improvements in everyday life to major advancements in the fields of art, science and economy. It is associated with personal well-being, and as automation and artificial intelligence increasingly outpace human intelligence, it is seen as an important future skill in both education and employment. Creativity is fascinating because it is often considered elusive and mysterious, as good ideas sometimes appear to come out of nowhere.

On the other hand, creativity is not special. We know that it is not limited to a few geniuses and is not exclusive to the arts. Everyone is endowed with the cognitive capacity to think creatively. It's an adaptive feature of the brain that developed long ago, as evidenced by early inventions, tools, and artefacts. Imagination refers to the human capacity to think of things we have never seen or heard of before; it allows us to transcend what we know and have experienced, and thus enables us to prepare for an uncertain future, to not only adapt but actively develop and shape this future. Artefacts like the lion-man of the Hohlenstein-Stadel (about 30,000 BC) highlight that we learned early on to combine known concepts in new ways, and even create counterfactual representations. This shows that imagination lets us go beyond the constraints of knowledge and reason, offering unlimited possibilities. Along these lines, many aspects of our brain functioning are not tuned towards maximizing efficiency or avoiding errors at all costs, but rather support plasticity and creativity.

It wasn't so long ago that psychology began to actively consider the importance of creativity. The first serious attempts to measure and study it happened about 70 years ago. Early work asked what cognitive process is engaged and what brain region is activated when people think creatively. Today we know it's not a single process or region. Creative ideas rely on ordinary (neuro)cognitive processes, ones that are also involved in other cognitive activities, but are configured in specific ways when we think creatively, and thereby recruit more or less the entire brain. I like to organize the central processes of human cognition into three aspects: memory, attention, and cognitive control. I will now share briefly what we have learnt about their role as elements of creative cognition.

Let's start with memory. At first glance, memory appears antithetical to creativity, because creative ideas must be novel by definition, and thus cannot simply be drawn from memory. However, creative ideas don't come from nowhere; they've been found to result from knowledge elements that are recombined or reconstructed in new and effective ways.

We can discriminate between two memory systems: semantic and episodic memory. Semantic memory reflects our knowledge about the world and is well organized. Episodic memory, on the other hand, refers to our personal, autobiographic experiences. Both memory systems offer unique pathways to understanding how new ideas are created.

For semantic memory, creative ideas result from finding links between unrelated concepts. For example, the words cottage, swiss, and cake appear unrelated until we identify that they are connected via the concept of cheese.

For episodic memory, creating works differently. Cognitive and neuroscientific work has shown that episodic memories are not drawn from a memory store as we would load an image from a hard drive. Rather, these memories are reconstructed from relevant memory elements. For example, my memory of seeing the Salzburg castle gets reconstructed from many previous experiences related to castles, hills, and cities. These reconstructions are never fully accurate, but this reconstruction machinery can also be applied to more creative forms of imagination. It lets us construct new representations that are built from available memory elements.

We can conclude that memory provides the building blocks for creative ideas. Vast amounts of evidence demonstrate how effective memory processes, such as retrieving and combining remote memory elements, support creative thinking. As creativity builds on memory, creative combinations are potentially limited by what elements are available. There is a tendency to recall well-known concepts better than weakly related ones, which can oppose creative thinking. Memory thus serves both as the foundation of creativity and as a potential constraint.

Let's move on to discussing the role of attention. Attention determines our current focus. As cognitive resources are very limited, there is only so much that we can focus on at a given time. In our research, we stumbled upon the importance of attention in brain studies using EEG (electroencephalography), which consistently revealed increased brain oscillations at a frequency of around 10 Hz, called alpha activity. We found that alpha activity was related to creativity in many ways. For instance, it increased when people engaged in more versus less creative tasks; when they had more creative ideas, alpha levels were higher in more creative people and even increased after creativity interventions. Other studies showed that alpha activity is not a "creativity wave", but right parietal alpha in particular indicates when people turn their attention inwardly, which is common during creative thinking involving imagination.

Imagination relies on internally directed attention. What we see and what we imagine in our mind's eye are different things that may interfere with each other. Here, alpha activity is thought to contribute to shielding our mental representations from irrelevant sensory interference. We can sometimes recognize this internal focus in others, as they "stare into space", deep in thought, averting their gazes, or even closing their eyes. We have begun to study eye behaviors, and thereby the brain activation, associated with internal attention. They show characteristic signs of perceptual decoupling from the environment and visual disengagement; still, pupil dilation indicates a high mental load during imagination.

Why is this relevant? Acknowledging the role of internal attention in creativity is important because we live in a very stimulus-driven world, with an abundance of interesting sensory information. Paying attention to these stimulations captures our thoughts and thus can potentially undermine self-generated, creative thinking. As someone with children, this concerns me a lot. I know how external stimulation can be highly gratifying and much less cognitively demanding than engaging in internally driven thinking. While such external stimulation can inspire us, internal attention supports imagination. The balance is key, as exclusive stimulus-driven mind states may not leave much room for one's own thoughts and ideas. Creative people actively ensure time and space for internal and self-driven focus in their daily routines.

This brings us to cognitive control. Creativity is often associated with spontaneity and a lack of control, but let's explore how this is studied in psychological research. According to dual-process models, cognition involves two types of processes: Spontaneous or Type 1 processes that are fast, automatic, undemanding, associative but also undirected; and controlled or Type 2 processes, which are slow, deliberate, effortful, analytical, and goal-directed. Both have their benefits. Type 1 processes are effortless and can handle large amounts of information at the same time, but only in an undirected, reflexive way; it gets tasks that require no conscious attention easily done. Type 2 processes allow us to direct our thoughts consciously. This is necessary to overcome dominant thoughts and perseveration. Importantly, Type 1 processes are always active, while Type 2 processes can be additionally activated.

In creativity research, we see evidence for the relevance of both processes. Spontaneous processes are evidenced in moments of spontaneous insight, such as during breaks or other times when we have not consciously worked on a task, and in activation of the default network of the brain. Conversely, we also see lots of evidence of how cognitive control supports creativity, specifically in terms of effective strategies, the robust association of creativity with executive control, intelligence, and the activation of the executive control network. Therefore, while spontaneous processes can do remarkable things, it's usually not a good idea to just sit and wait until they get the creative work done, but rather advisable to additionally engage in controlled thinking, or at least ensure shifts between phases of lower and higher control.

We can take away that creativity is at least partly under our control, which is good news. However, this also implies that creative thinking, while many enjoy it, can also be very effortful and cognitively demanding. As such, it needs to be valued and supported accordingly.

To sum up, we begin to understand how creative ideas arise from the interplay of cognitive elements including memory, attention and cognitive control processes. Creativity builds on memory, is supported by internal attention, and is partly under control. Knowing the cognitive elements underlying creative cognition will help us to better support creativity in ourselves, as well as in others.

6. Creativity of Artists

Josh Miller, MBA, Co-Founder & CEO of IDEAS xLab and Owner of Josh Miller Ventures

Before I dive into the work we do at IDEAS xLab, I'll start by sharing a little bit about my artistic practice and my experience with the Creativity of Artists. I'm a queer photographer and entrepreneur, and for over a decade have used photography to explore the world as I run, hike and cycle.

Early on in COVID-19, I began printing my photography as silk and chiffon prints – which I call Wearable Photos™ - offered through my business Josh Miller Ventures. I create them to unleash a new way of showing up in the world – you're creating an art installation each time you wear them! My current collections feature images from Kentucky and Colorado, available in square prints, draped cardigans, and more.

The "Golden Hour" silk Wearable Photos™ print I wear as a scarf, for example, is a mirrored image long-exposure photo of the sunrise in Colorado from the trails in the front range. It just so happens to match the Sonophilia Foundation logo! That's just one way that creativity presents itself in my life – which is also infused into my public speaking and storytelling – all of which inform our work at IDEAS xLab.

IDEAS xLab is the artist-led nonprofit I co-founded with my husband Theo Edmonds that uses the art of storytelling and community collaboration to impact public health.

Our organization is almost 10 years old and has worked on projects that leverage creativity and innovation with more than 95 artists from six countries and 10 public health researchers since our launch in Louisville, KY.

Creativity is one of our core values - whether it comes in the form of poetry or photography, or the larger efforts that bridge our lived experiences, work across sectors and artistic practices to change policy and encourage new ways of working and thinking.

We know that cultural context and re-envisioning how people are engaged are important for impacting public health, cultivating hope and strengthening people's sense of belonging.

Our organization's journey has included testing out a variety of organizational structures and ways of working- pulling from backgrounds like Theo Edmonds's experience in healthcare, my MBA, and Hannah Drake's work as an activist and author. I'm going to share a few initiatives that have been part of that journey; each represents different ways that we - as artists - have infused creativity into our work.

XLerateArt was an effort supported by the National Endowment for the Arts where we engaged artists in corporate residence with companies in the United States including a health insurer and General Electric's maker space and micro-factory - FirstBuild.

One example was our collaboration with Polish artist and architect Jakub Szczęsny. He worked with GE's FirstBuild to engage the community and create what he called The Louisville Table, a social appliance that allows people to stand together around the table and cook a meal. During the process, he asked the engineers if the machines could cut the wood and work in specific ways they hadn't considered before. It was this artistic infusion that opened up opportunities for them to expand their processes and maximize what their machines could do.

Another effort, which started in 2017, was One Poem At A Time. In response to the community's priority of beautification, my team member Hannah asked, "What if we changed each negative billboard, one poem at a time?" We took photos of community members and worked with them to write one-sentence poems - all to envision a change in the environment with an eye toward policy change. The policy focus shifted when the community needed it to - focusing on licenses for businesses wanting to sell alcohol. It was amazing to see how an artist-led effort supported a policy change across the city while defeating the liquor license applications.

That first campaign launched our ongoing partnership with the Louisville Metro Department of Public Health & Wellness. It used our artist-led approach to work with the community to create culturally responsive messaging with the latest billboard series on childhood lead poisoning prevention and COVID-19 performing at 233% above industry standard for click-through rates for the digital billboard/ad. This type of creative approach is changing how they think about working with community members to create public health messaging.

In 2019-2020, we wanted to explore whether we could impact the hope and sense of belonging of students and young people through artist-led collaborations focused on topics the young people were interested in - pride, identity, and bullying.

We worked with Theo's team on the research, and over two years, implemented a series of arts activities with the young people from a middle school and LGBTQ+ youth group - from poetry exercises and designing t-shirts to the creation of an iMovie called "A War on Us: It's All Bullying."

When Covid disrupted the process, canceling the premiere of the iMovie and the event planned by the LGBTQ+ youth group, we pivoted to hosting some virtual convenings. The students found new ways to finish their film remotely and worked together with our artist team to host the "We the Youth: Our Emotional Wellbeing

Summit". When we released the Belonging Through Creative Arts Activity Book - available for free online at ideasxlab.com/activitybook - we found that even through a pandemic, 60% of youth who participated in multiple measurement points over time experienced an increase in hope and belonging scores through the project.

Building on that work and our experiences across sectors, Hannah and I saw an opportunity for using activities and processes we'd developed to lead inclusion, diversity, equity and accessibility workshops and consulting.

What we created over the past few years are ways to bypass and adapt outdated mental models by utilizing arts-based hands-on and interactive activities, internal reflection, and small and large group discussions to best support the different ways people process information and form new ways of seeing the world. Artists help corporate teams and nonprofits move their organizations forward through workshops, strategy development and consulting.

Our primary effort right now is (Un)Known Project, which uses art installations and experiences to honor the names and tell the stories of enslaved Black people in Louisville, KY and beyond.

Through IDEAS xLab, Hannah, Theo and I have worked in Natchez, MS and traveled together to Senegal, West Africa. These journeys helped us see how much of the history of enslavement in Kentucky had been intentionally hidden or erased. Louisville is one of the most segregated cities in the US – and we believed that it would take multiple interactions with the project to reach many different parts of the community. To do this, we created public art installations like On the Banks of Freedom and unearthed more than 150 names (as of early 2022) of enslaved people through the project. The names are engraved on the granite backs of the benches, with the footprints of Black Louisvillians along the edge of the platform representing enslaved people facing Indiana – a free state when Kentucky was a slave state.

In June 2022, multiple commissioned art pieces were unveiled by our museum partners along with the premiere of our immersive Journeys to Freedom: (Un)Known Project River Cruise, which features the stories of two families seeking to escape enslavement by boat across the Ohio River.

(Un)Known Project is becoming a series of thematically connected sites throughout the US, as we continue to work with communities to leverage creativity to transform how they relate to their history and shared future.

As you can see through these examples, artists - beyond painting a mural or creating a sculpture - are using their creativity to change our communities, the stories they tell, and how they work together and value culture. We are working at the intersection of arts and culture, community engagement, innovation, and research. It has been amazing to see what can happen when we envision and bring into the world these much-needed pathways for change and impact.

Visit ideasxlab.com to learn more about our work.

7. Reimagining The Creative Industries

Bernd Fesel, Interim Chief Executive Officer of the EIT Culture & Creativity

As someone who has been involved in the creative industry for many years, I always say 'you can go to work without a car or a plane, but not without culture and creativity.' We dress in fashion every day, consume news and storytelling via the radio, television, or social media, and listen to music regularly. We live in buildings, sometimes in Cultural Heritage, and sit at tables and chairs: architecture and furniture design are around us every hour. Millions use all the products of the cultural and creative industries every day, sometimes even every hour or minute. And yet, with each small decision, they are creating global markets of vast amounts, e.g in fashion: € 1.900 Billion. At the same time, these decisions are such a daily habit that they are almost invisible. It's nearly impossible to go about our daily lives without at least some of these cultural and creative products.

The term Creative Industries is a relatively new one, e.g first coined by the German Federal government in 2008, with quite nuanced and fresh implications in the field of creative research. Many economic researchers and some politicians argued at that time that it was not a sector in itself, but rather a developing field. They wondered, and still wonder, what the creative industries are. Well, to offer a glimpse into this massive international business, let's take a look at some numbers and data.

The creative industries have an approximate global value of one trillion dollars, which to put it into perspective, is 10% of the global GDP by 2030. The year 2021 was announced as the very first United Nations global year of creativity and innovation, and from this policy initiative, we were able to explore specific sectors, like design – particularly interface design – where we saw a staggering 158 billion downloads globally. We also have a global culture of gaming with 2.5 billion gamers, as well as a fashion market worth billions.

Creativity is also a young dynamic business in Europe. There are some 30,000 novel companies every year, and a venture capital market of 30 billion others that have been game changers, many of which were nurtured and grew out of Europe, such as King Soopers and Spotify. With all these investments and innovations in many of these companies every year, I believe that while we witness a young dynamic of early adoptions of societal trends, there's also a certain air of tradition inherent in the making of emerging markets. This then leads to the question of what kind of business creativity is, which comes up with those staggering amounts of turnover and involvement.

The European Parliament adopted 2016 a resolution on European coherent policies for cultural and creative industries. In their latest definition, these are the industries that rely on culture and creative inputs based on cultural values, diversity, individual or collective creativity, and skills and talent with the potential to generate innovation, wealth and jobs. This definition tends to prioritize the creation of social value over economic value, so the contribution of cultural creative industries to society is much larger than the turn of the aforementioned numbers. One of the ongoing scientific tasks is to show this societal contribution to other sectors as well.

How do we understand these broader impacts of culture & creativity? How do we measure them? Forming those statistics definitions are extremely important for us to be inclusive and open to new artistic developments. When I was the vice director at the European Capital of Culture RUHR.2010, we encouraged artists and creators to participate in debates about these definitions, that is their self-understanding. Even if they seem extremely boring and far away from the real-life problems of artists, they are still highly relevant in framing the future for artists.

In the last few years, however, the cultural and creative sectors have expanded, now employing some 9 million people. Creativity as a skill, though, goes far beyond those sectors. In 2019, the European Commission discovered that some 2 million companies outside of the creative industries are driven by creativity as a major income stream. In comparison, there are about 3 million companies within the creative industries. We have some 9 million jobs within the creative industries, while some 33 million jobs are driven by the skill of creativity outside of the CCSI. On top of value chains and production crossing sectors, markets start to merge, making sector-specific definitions somewhat obsolete, though we can not do without them.

It is important to note that the COVID-19 pandemic has hit our sector rather heavily, with the total turnover falling by 31% in the EU. The crisis has been strongest in central and eastern Europe, particularly in Germany and Italy, where more than half of the creative industries in the whole of Europe have been growing very slowly. The formerly high-growth markets in the Eastern US, unfortunately, have also been hit hard by the COVID crisis.

To offer a glimpse into what the European Union plans to do to foster creativity, there is an audio-visual media action plan, as well as a mission for climate adaptation, health and soil including CCSI. Also, the Renovation Wave want to speed up the green transformation of the construction sector. Other sector-specific calls are, for example, fashion and music. Furthermore, a funding program within Horizon Europe called Cluster 2 "Culture, Creativity and Inclusive Society" has newly started in 2021. There's also a program supporting small and medium-sized companies. Finally, funding programs from the European Innovation Bank support public-private matching funds.

On top of all those programs, you have funding from the National COVID Recovery

Plans. A survey of ECBN shows that 17 of 27 nations included Creative Industries in their programs, summing up to a staggering amount of € 6 - 7 B. That is a sound basis to contribute to the digital green transformation and make Europe a carbon-neutral continent. With all this in mind, I would say it's the golden age of our sectors because there has never been so much programming and funding from the European Union.

Now let's have a look at how this infiltrates politics. Even before the definition in 2016 was made by the European Union, there was a research project initiated by my European creative business network on what the economic effects of the cultural creative industries might be within our sector and beyond. The spill-over effects and the systems involved were broken down into three pillars: knowledge spill-overs, industry spill-overs, and network spill-overs. Together with Arts Council England, as well as several universities, Nesta, and some 20 partners forming a European Research Alliance, we looked into how to monitor and evaluate those aspects of the cultural and creative sectors and industries, and supplemented this topic with some 100 studies, looking at the tools in those studies.

We discovered that there are hardly any tools that look for qualitative, long-term monitoring. Usually, monitoring stops when the funding of the project stops, which is much too short. We are now hopeful for the start of an Innovation Agency for Europe to rebalance the tools for creative industries, create more tools for qualitative research on CCSI, and implement a more balanced research agenda for creative industries. To learn more, have a look at the Joint Research Center, which operates the only "Cultural and Creative Cities Monitor" in Europe.

Creativity is now also mainstreamed into economic policy. The European Union selected CCSI to be one of its 14 industrial ecosystems critical for its industrial strategy. I was invited into those working groups of the European Commission to debate and negotiate on this topic. Over the next seven years, our sector has a wonderful chance - and obligation - to contribute to this industrial strategy, as well as focus on climate neutrality and digital leadership. I don't particularly believe that our sector culture and creative industries are ready to do so, as many of them are just focusing on tackling their day-to-day problems. Creative Industries must change, now more than ever, to live up to this challenge and this opportunity to be part of Europe's industrial strategy!

Additionally, creativity prevails in climate change and education policies. It was a highly discussed topic at the last COP 26, where the Italian government, as part of the G20 nations, highlighted the UN climate action. Where education is concerned, there is the Creative Pact4Skills initiative whereby upskilling and reskilling our sector is prioritized. The European Union recently announced a major funding project that highlights skills for the Creative Industries. This will help in the creation of new curricula for vocational training, as well as for new master's and new bachelor's degrees.

As you can see, the topics of culture and creative industries within the last 10 years have seeped into many different sectors. I believe understanding creativity through a scientific lens, not just an economic one, is key. We can all agree that it's not just good business for a carbon-based society, but also for a post-carbon society. If you look into the industrial change in the last 20 or 25 years, our main approach in the creative industries to drive change through skills was design thinking. Tim Brown, who serves as the CEO of the innovation and design firm IDEO, is a famous evangelist. He takes design thinking as a human-centered approach to innovation and mainstreams this into the industry. He believes in user-centered creative deployment, driving innovation, whether it's design thinking in the organization and business capabilities or the link of innovation activity to the market. Design thinking is also a source of competitive advantage.

I now ask: What is the next step for creative skill? Our understanding of design thinking so far might come to an end with an industrial change in the circular economy. The circular economy demands a change of value chains and sectors in parallel, as well as an abundance of details that are quite difficult to grasp and organize. While design thinking has been iterative and works in loops across sectors, we might realize that the classical design thinking iterative game needs to be further developed and improved. Be creative about design thinking and consider where we go from there.

Some artists and architects are already doing this. Take, for example, Kalavati Somvanshi, an architect and inventor in many dimensions of new materials, who looks at the new use of buildings. Other Architects like Bjarke Ingels, a big group that's not just reinventing the use of buildings, but also the use of the cityscape of the whole urban surrounding, reimagining the social fabric and how we interrelate in those spaces. Last but not least, a gaming project - Games Forest Club - took up the challenge of planting trees globally, uniting and focusing on the social capacity of some 2.5 billion gamers around the globe. It turns the fun motivation of being creative in your free time and repurposes it for a social cause on a global scale. Imagine what would happen if just 2% of 2.5 billion users focused on one thing: restoring life to the natural world. This is the kind of cross-sectorial value creation the circular economy approach calls for.

Let's take circular thinking beyond the design thinking of Tim Brown. Suppose we want to contribute as a sector to a sustainable economy. In that case, we need a new tool to envision and imagine this new future to take consumers, customers, people, citizens, students, pupils, professors, etc. along with us. I believe this tool must be empirically based, as well as data-based. The latest developments I see here are the digital twin development, which takes new futures in both calculation models and simulation models. Visual simulations increase understanding if they're data-based. In the circular economy, so many parallel changes are happening that if you do not put them in a visual, easy-to-grasp story, we will not be able to take people along adequately. Not even policymakers will understand the future they are creating through all the regulations they are changing in parallel. Creativity, which could be used to shape a more calm, free future might not have the desired outcome.

Historically, wall paintings in churches took people along; the wall paintings of today are simulations in games. Today artists are using coding as a new tool to "paint the future."

I believe we gathered for this Creativity Congress for this very reason: to bring together all these different disciplines. This gives me hope that I'm not alone in envisioning this future. I imagine technologies upskilled for creativity will be transformed into creative tools, and I hope those simulations will then become conveyor belts to that desired future.

8. SPACE MATTERS: The Architecture of Creativity

Gitte Andersen, Author, Professional Board Member & Founder of GA Consulting – The workplace Faculty

I define creativity as democratic, diverse, sustainable, inclusive, experimental, a team effort, and fun.

The architecture of creativity is something I've spent the last 25 years working with, having authored four books on the connection between space and behavior – both concerning workplaces and learning environments. (www.GAconsulting.dk) Originally, I was educated as an architect at the Royal Academy of Art in Copenhagen and later studied economics. After founding my own consulting company, I sold it to a global Workplace Facility Service company from where I worked around the world, and now I'm back to just being myself. I still advise global companies about the future of work and how the design of space can promote creativity and innovation – all based on data and evidence.

Space Is Never Neutral.

Space will always either hinder or promote our successes, whether it is our learning environment, our working environment, our culture, our buildings, or our communities. Wherever we are, we exist in spaces that either limit or promote creativity and collaboration among people. Space is never neutral. Therefore, it's important and relevant to observe how different designs of space can promote the way people collaborate, innovate, communicate, and be creative together.

A creative-thinking world must comprise all kinds of people. If we can agree that there is no one-size-fits-all when it comes to designing our learning environments or working environments, we must also acknowledge that people's needs and ways of doing things are different. Focusing on a design that leaves space for diversity is a necessity.

Consider this quote by Matt Adams: "With creativity, we stop relying on what's always been and open our eyes to what might be." Architects must also begin their designs from the inside out. Similarly, Jenn Maer said, "When you think creatively, you're opening your heart and mind and you're relating to people as humans." We need to understand people's needs, and from there, give them the best spaces to develop their creativity.

My focus has primarily been to look into all the existing spaces we already have and try to figure out how we can upgrade, transform, and convert them into something that supports creativity much more than they did when they were originally built. Of course, getting funding for new architecture is fantastic, but the world is already filled with buildings. If we don't start to use them in another way, we will fall behind in developing new creative ideas and it will become a prison for us in our creativity.

At the same time, our world is rife with individualism and social differences, volatility and increased cultural fragmentation. The world is crying for creativity, the capacity to wonder and ask questions, astonishment and readiness, opportunities to learn, cohesiveness, and for creative power so we can come up with solutions for the future's challenges. In a welfare economy on a diet and new requirements for future learning and working environments, we need to focus more on all our existing resourcefulness and how we can activate that in new ways!

Our Buildings In The Sharing Economy.

I have collected data on the use of learning and working environments over the last 20 years, doing anthropological studies, both on the quantitative and the qualitative sides. Where is it always empty? Where's it always lively? Where do the informal meetings take place? Where does collaboration take place? Where do people sit alone? On average, when you look at grade schools, professional schools and universities, 50% of our M2 is standing empty during the day, and if you look at their use during evenings, the vacancy rate is even higher. The number of unused square meters is ridiculous.

Because people move around a lot, you never see the same empty M2. Many of our buildings have been built for a monofunctional use, where work was a space and not an activity. We keep our private ownership to M2 even if we do not use them. Therefore, many M2 are left alone, ready to be activated to new diverse spaces promoting creativity! This pattern goes across working and learning environments, in public municipalities and administrative buildings, etc.

I believe we need to look at all the unused square meters and buildings in a sharing economy way, which would allow us a fresh perspective on how to activate them in new ways.

As an example, I observed a lot of company headquarters and analyzed all the facilities they could share with others in a co-working environment or several user houses. This analysis showed that an average of 17% to 29% of the total gross area each company headquarter had could be shared with others. Imagine what would happen if we started to share these facilities not only as a reduced Eco footprint but also as a working community, where we start to engage, to co-create, to co-work, to open the doors to the local community and work together. Here, sharing could be the enabler for promoting creativity and helping to make creativity flourish – just by sharing facilities.

The Flourishing Of Creativity Starts When We Are Born.

Focusing on the next generation, we need to ask ourselves: what skillset is necessary for the 21st century to deal with future challenges? Do we know what kind of job titles the future requires? It could be a digital tailor, garbage designer, drone traffic controller, virtual reality influencer, genetic AI biologist, climate GEO engineer, ethical algorithm programmer, meat lab scientist, or free-time experience planner.
What kind of competencies should we ensure the next generation have? Could it have to do with knowledge? Will skills like interdisciplinarity, traditional (i.e mathematics), modern (i.e. entrepreneurship), or themes (i.e. global literacy) be what's most important to know and understand?

Perhaps it will be about character – how we behave and engage in the world. In that case, skills like mindfulness, curiosity, courage, resilience, ethics, and leadership would be key.

Skills may be the most prominent competency to possess and how we use what we know. Creativity, critical thinking, communication, and collaboration may take precedence. We must improvise, asphalt the road while driving on it and make space for all kinds of thinking.

At the same time, the how and where of learning is exploding - you can learn anything, anywhere, anytime with more or less anyone, from classroom teaching to lectures to self-studies to e-learning to crowd curses to flipped learning to group work to mentoring to project-based to game-based to challenged-based to online/off-line to phenomenon-based to experience-based. The list goes on and on.

The Mental Rebuild *

When looking at the design of the learning environments we have, for example, a ground school, you can see the normal old classroom setting in rows as we know it – with the teacher as a one-way communicator on the blackboard. Or, we could take the same classroom, change the settings and inventory as a shared diverse space, and split it into three different scenarios that support different ways of learning: from framework teaching to group work, from diversified teaching to workshops. We needn't move walls or rebuild to promote creative learning. This is a mental rebuild, and we can do it tomorrow. We have another way of teaching.

It's about transforming the many unused M2 into spaces for design thinking - incoherent learning environments with mediation rooms, study rooms, supervision rooms, experimentation rooms and exercise rooms. It's about designing space for Fab Lab makerspace, where we can create ideas for what might be in the future.
The future may be more concerned with what we do together than what we own individually. I did a global study on three universities in New York, three in India and three in the UK just before the pandemic, in which I engaged with a lot of students

about great places to work. On average, 77% of them said they would rather spend money on an authentic experience among people that were present than buy a product.

My generation has filled our homes with designer furniture and art -- things you can touch. However, the next generation has a sustainable mindset – planet first, then people and purpose! How can we make sure that all the world's companies transform into a much more sustainable production without giving the people inside them the skills to make this big transformation possible?

Space Matters

Research has shown us that we already know a lot about how the design of space can promote creativity. For example, physical activity makes children smarter. Researchers say that the muscles speak to the brain. What if we open the door, go outside and do sports and all kinds of activities to foster the brain with other people rather than have it be a solitary experience? Consider an Outdoor School. Are you living close to a sea, a forest, a beach, a parking lot, or a playing ground? Going outside to investigate all the gold in the neighborhood could stimulate children's curiosity to discover. Exploring the marvellous world we are all part of, asking such questions as Where does hail come from? How are soap bubbles made? How does the water come out of the faucet? Why does liquid come out of my eyes when I cry and am sad? Why is the moon sometimes out during the day? How are water puddles made? How can a fish live underwater? How does light enter the lamps?

The Future Of Work

Let's envision a future that is more flexible, productive, inclusive, sustainable, collaborative, ageless, mindful, intuitive – but mostly, much healthier and more fun! Talk of the workplace has found its way into all people's minds. We just witnessed the largest workplace experiment and global transformation to virtual work ever during the Covid19 pandemic. We have certainly learned a lot from that experience.

If the pandemic has taught us anything, it's that employees crave investment in the human aspects of work. Employees are tired and many are grieving. They want a renewed and revised sense of purpose in their work. They want social and interpersonal connections with their colleagues and managers. They want to feel a sense of shared identity. Yes, they want pay, benefits, and perks, but they also want to feel valued by their organisations and managers. They want meaningful interactions, not just transactions.

Working from home showed us an alternative to how we can work – we want to keep the increased flexibility and individual choices for where to work, and we certainly want less time spent commuting every day, which can directly be invested in "my time" or family time and a new place for the focused deep dive solitary work. We also recognized the challenges that come with only having the work-from-home option. The Top Five challenges of working from home are lack of socialization with colleagues, lack of collaboration with colleagues, a decreased sense of belonging – both professionally and socially, and therefore, for some, an increased sense of loneliness – all of which could inevitably lead to a great lack of creativity!

Working from home will undoubtedly remain an option from here on out, as will other hybrid Hub format solutions, but the office is not a dead space. Quite the contrary, during the pandemic we greatly felt the importance of the office. Now is the time to rethink the purpose of the office as the number one place for unplugged work to occur, to feel the passion and pulse among people present – those who, like you, have taken the trip to the office.

Leaders now have the chance to come back stronger than before the pandemic and ask themselves: How do we create authentic, diverse, creative and inclusive workplaces where talent flourishes across ages, where we are all part of a force for good and making the world work better? We must focus on a sustainable life-work-learn balance – something the generations entering the work life now will demand, expect and look for! Let's put people, pulse, and passion back in the office space!

Purpose Before Profit!

There are now four demographic/generations in the workplace. Gen. Z is the first generation to prioritise purpose over money, more concerned with personal values and a new moral compass for good work which has begun to develop. We want to know what good our daily work does in the world. We expect that meaning will be placed above profit, which will probably come if the organisation does well with what it releases into the world – especially in relation to sustainability. It's a merger between workstyles and lifestyles.

Lifelong Learning

A company's capacity to learn determines its capacity to adapt and, ultimately, its chances of surviving far into the future. If your company isn't learning, it isn't growing.

Though 95% of companies responding to a BCG survey agreed that corporate learning was crucial to the future of the company and should be considered a high priority, only 15% said they had delivered on this priority, simply because it's hard to do so. The survey also predicted that 60% of workers will need to be reskilled or upskilled over the next two to five years. Creative systems thinking, high social competencies, entrepreneurial mindset and working with complexity may all be desirable attributes across most industries.

At the same time, we will see the rise of a new generation entering the job market with a free agent mindset, building up their curriculum, flying from project to project according to what inspires them and helps their development. This is a generation that wants to learn from the best. They do not see their lives split into three ages – that is, one where we study and learn, one where we work, and finally one where we retire. This generation expects life-long learning and continuous progress in skills and competencies; the appetite for learning is voracious. Different research studies state that around 59% of the jobs that will be done in 15 years haven't even been invented yet.

Turn Your Company into a Learning Powerhouse.

Some talk about "The Organisational Health" as a definition of the ability and capability to want to change through acquiring new competencies. This will be what differentiates successful top candidates from others – the ability to transform and ensure that candidates not only fit in now but also in the future, with great creative mindsets!

It is also key to look at life-long learning not only as a one-off, short-term upskilling initiative, but leaders in corporate education must build distinctive, creative, sustainable, digital, and physical learning ecosystems. Ensuring that the hybrid work format – at the office, at home or in the Hub – all deliver great ongoing upskilling and learning opportunities.

The Gen Z workforce is a creative global problem-solving curious generation – with a strong desire for a new educational model that includes a blend of virtual and in-person learning, true-to-life work experiences and mentorship, future-focused curriculum and greater levels of creativity and self-direction. They prefer greater exposure to real-life work and professional mentorship, and they see both the education community and large businesses as the primary institutions responsible for preparing them for the future of work.

What does that workplace look like? For sure, the workplace design looks different than what we see today, and it is certainly not something we can leave to chance. After all, SPACE MATTERS!

People Above Workplace

For many years, we thought about THE WORKPLACE as a DESIGN discipline rather than a set of methods and ideas to support and promote business performance. This has also been the case for me as an educated architect.

As a natural consequence of the themes mentioned in this chapter, the perceived wisdom is now challenged and changing to a new people-centric starting point, ensuring that we create workplaces to connect people and places with great experiences - both on a professional level and a personal one. This won't be easy, because it requires companies and their leaders to truly understand their employees. It also requires leaders to develop much deeper empathy for what employees are going through and to pair that empathy with compassion and determination to act and change.

Our new challenge is to be able to meet the individual as they are and where they are in life. This is about understanding the whole employee journey from brand building, onboard learning and development, happy exit, alumni, staying in touch and coming back. It's about not just zooming in on a one size fits all "normal" workday at the office, but rather building long-term loyalty instead of fighting against the retention agenda we may already have lost! The future is about keeping all the good stuff up to speed, and growing relationships between existing and previous colleagues in alumni networking, communities, clubhouses, lectures and recurring events.

People are different, workstyles differ, where we are in life varies; spaces should also be different! Let's celebrate our diversity and opportunities and start working with them rather than against them. Collaboration and diversity are about putting people first!

What's ART Got To Do With It?

A major Danish art museum just had a group of artists exhibit pieces on the theme of the future of work, called "Work it out". Many of the pieces offer us "mind juice" for a more people-centric approach to work and the spaces where it takes place – especially an installation called "We are having the time of our lives". This piece combined humor with a critical perspective: the X factor we put on top of work, workplace hacks, and our thoughts on what could make it better. Our people-centric workplaces could be much more diverse, balanced, creative, flexible, productive, inclusive, sustainable, collaborative, ageless, mindful and intuitive – but most importantly, they could be much more fun workplaces in the future!

"Spontaneity is a keyword for us. It rhymes with energy and flow. And for us to be able to work like that we need to keep our setup and maintenance fairly simple. This setup is not to be confused with small or unambitious initiatives."
Quote; **JIR SANDEL** - an artist-run gallery and champion of decentralised exhibition making.

9. Art & Science Of Courageous Imagination

Theo Edmonds, Co-Curator of CACC, JD, MHA, MFA, Culture Futurist ™

Close your eyes for a second. I want you to imagine someone in your life who deeply matters to you.

What if every decision you made as a professional was in that person's best interest? How might your day-to-day choices be different? This is how it feels to inhabit a story of "us"—something bigger than just one person. A tale of courageous imagination that, since the beginning of human time, has been true.

If we go back far enough, all human knowledge began as imagination. It started with the first time someone looked up at the stars and thought, "I wonder what that's all about." This is an instinct to know the unknown. Let's think of this as our "head" instinct.

There is another instinct, too, that pulses through us. We feel it when we're with our friends. The state of feeling like we matter and are connected to others. The instinct to belong. The well-being instincts of the "heart".

And, finally, there is the instinct of our "hands". Even in nature, we see it as trees intertwining with the forest around them. The instinct to have autonomy and self-determination, but, at the same time, to join with others to do more together than any one of us can do alone.

These are the instincts that guide our imagination. In connecting our head, heart, and hands, we synchronize our internal and external experience of the world.
Over this morning's CACC presentations, we've heard a lot of stories: scientific stories, data stories, and money stories. But the question I have for you today is the same one that artist Raghava KK posed to the audience in their 2020 Boma presentation: "Can we live the best story that we can tell?"

Our world is in a lot of pain right now. We often discuss pain points and gain points in designing for innovation. I want to use a different technique to help us understand data: The cultural intelligence process called poetry. This is one of my own.

There is a secret painful and lonely wisdom that comes
from being a cool wet seed in hot scorched earth.
Caught between mud brick and flame
Caught between moonlight and Tesla cars,
Caught between running and clutching
A cool wet seed turning into hot scorched earth.
Revealing imaginative truths of Pharisees and merchant kings
to be seen for what they are.
Wet bones standing in bloody
shoes. A dream of fire.
A baby with a swollen belly.
A child looking at us from a puzzled soul who takes
notice of the emperor's new clothes.
It is a child brave enough to ask the only question
which truly scares us.
Why do some, we ask, want to be rulers everywhere?
(Inescapably, we know that we are all mirrors and windows.)
A tender voice sneaks up on us
Conjuring memories from before knowledge
Before the time we followed others
who wanted us to believe
that we have words to name
flowers. A time of imagination.
A time of wonder.
As we sit in this room,
Memory still stirs our future.
For in this very present
moment, A new, wet seed
begins to turn.
Courage. Reaching to touch the light.

Perhaps unlike the experiences of my European colleagues, being American is a unique idea, not a lineage. E Pluribus Unum. Out of many, one. One nation that has commodified healthcare and education as much as we have bread.

Time, too, has been commodified. We "spend time" doing this. We "pay attention" to that. Most Americans will spend more hours of their waking life at work than anywhere else.

In the workplace, the Great Resignation is a story we tell -- millions of people leaving their jobs at a pace never before seen in our history. Toxic work culture is the number one reason that people are leaving.

It's not just our private sector economy at risk, but also our essential institutions. America's healthcare system was already stressed before the COVID-19 pandemic. During COVID, one in five health workers quit their jobs. Our population is aging. Americans over 65 years old, those with the highest need for medical care, will jump exponentially as a percentage of our overall population. This will stress America's health system even further. My friend Carol Graham at the Brookings Institute, who does a lot of work on well-being in the American context, has documented that declining well-being is even becoming a national security issue.

When it comes to education, one in four American teachers are not just planning to quit their jobs; they are considering leaving the teaching profession entirely in search of more meaningful employment.

A healthy, intergenerational, diverse ecosystem of creativity is needed now more than at any time in the past 50 years. Globally, creative industries employ more young people between the ages of 18 and 25 than any other industry. But, in the creative industries' fastest growing areas, like gaming, 75% of the world's game developers are white and only around 8% of the main characters in video games are women of color. This suggests that the industry is not benefiting from contributions by all its stakeholders.

In America, despite the technological advancement, many of our systems still linger in much of the old industrial economy that, for over 100 years, trained us all to sit in rooms and listen to someone talk at us from the front of a room.

Our young people don't buy into this though. With or without us, they are using courage and imagination to bring about change that makes sense for their lives. The Gen Z doesn't plan on working the same job all their lives. Many don't even plan on staying in the same profession or the same industry throughout the talent development arc of their human experience.

By most any metric, one thing is clear. Americans like their paycheck. We can be clear on that but work itself is misaligned with our human instincts that make work meaningful.

Research on the environmental conditions of creativity reveals something important. Diverse lived experiences, like being part of the BIPOC or LGBTQ+ community, create opportunities to gain novel insights into the world. These insights come from navigating through dominant cultures, not designed with diverse perspectives in mind. In navigating these systems many of us are often forced to hide important parts of ourselves. Sometimes for career advancement. Sometimes, just to be safe.

In navigating, we begin developing learned, earned, skills known as cognitive flexibility. The World Economic Forum names this among the top skills for the future of work.

Take caution here, though. When a person is forced to do this to advance on the job or to maintain stability in their lives, it causes chronic tension to build. This, in turn, causes inflammation in the body which has been causally related to some forms of cancer and heart disease.

Putting this deleterious health impact aside for the moment, the cognitive flexibility skill set does something else. These skills cause creativity, curiosity, compassion, and more to develop in profound and fascinating ways. These skills expand opportunities for novel ideas to surface. To turn a novel idea into a valuable enterprise-wide asset, research suggests that there needs to be a perceived alignment between the motivations of the group of employees who brought forward the idea and the motivations of the employer. Inclusion can be helpful for companies to establish this alignment.

Inclusion is the key to unlocking the next wave of innovation in our society. At the University of Colorado Denver, we have been working over the last year to launch a new initiative called the Imaginator Academy.

Imaginator Academy is set on becoming an influential, quantitative analytics and innovation hub for culture futurism and creativity strategy. Strengthening the intersection of arts, science, and business in the future of work is our convergent goal.

From our base camp in the Rocky Mountains, we are connecting a global network of entrepreneurs, companies, scientists, artists, creatives, innovators, and change-makers of all kinds to transform research insights into cultural intelligence for solving business challenges centered on the human experience. We are finding incredible new ways to leverage the emerging science of creativity, social well-being, and collaboration to make the **future of work—WORK FOR ALL!**

Being an imagination engine for the future of work, there are three engagement focus areas with companies.

Culture Analytics, Strategy, and Research.

Our data-supported approach uses scientific methods to visualize where there are hidden opportunities to improve the social well-being of teams and emerging opportunities to foster inclusive innovation in industries.

Creativity Infrastructure Development

As we've seen here today, creativity is all around us. It's essential to the human experience. We find it in the arts, sciences, humanities, entrepreneurship, and all facets of life, but companies must be able to understand it, measure it and manage it in order to benefit .

Creativity can feel threatening to some, but creativity is only dangerous if you don't know how to use it. We are experts at ciphering through the research noise to identify creativity skills gaps across diverse sectors. We bring "what works" from evidence-based research to upskill a company's creativity infrastructure. Giving a company its best shot at producing new economic or social value from its latent creative capacity is what Imaginator Academy is designed to do in a culturally responsive way.

Culture Foresight Consultancy

While nobody can predict the future, our work is evidence-based and defensible. We translate a broad range of research and creative work into customized coaching to equip diverse leaders with the skills they need to improve the culture readiness of their companies and transform novel, good ideas into enterprise-wide value.

From a diffusion of innovation standpoint, we deploy resources to identify and invest in "early adopters". These are people who are motivated by change itself. Diffusion of innovation research show these are the wonder-bringers, the group who "de-risk" innovation for others. This is what those in the majority are looking for to join any culture change movement. And, let's be clear, innovation is more about culture change than most any other thing.

For more than a decade, I've been working towards something I would now like to share publicly for the first time: Courageous Imagination—a quantitative set of measurable data signals that visualize a company's capacity and readiness for inclusive innovation.

The data signals pull from population health science, organizational psychology, management research, neuroscience, and more. Together, forming a series of three nested, measurable human experiences that align culture change with innovation. First, we seek to understand a group's Creativity Capital (head instincts) or capacity for coming up with novel ideas.

Second, we assess a group's Social Wellbeing Capital (heart instincts), or its readiness to work together in transforming its creativity into new, enterprise-wide value. The data signals of metrics around compassion, awe, hope, trust, belonging, self-determination, and so on help us to understand this.

Third, we assess the Collaboration Capital (hands instincts), or what processes a group uses in its innovation efforts and how well these processes align with the greater socio-cultural context in a company's external operating environment. Context matters immensely for any innovation. But, it is one least considered by most companies. Collaboration Capital includes five core areas of analysis: Social Intention; Trustworthy storytelling and media; Analytics that people can use; Generational values alignment; and Environments supporting creativity.

Many systems today are still working in the imagination and vestiges of 100-year-old economies that were built to serve historical hierarchies. Perhaps we need to be asking a different set of questions. Rather than asking how might we tinker with a sunset, maybe we should be asking what if there are horizons we haven't yet conceived? This is a question of wonder, awe, curiosity and humility. Not one of certainty and bravado, two illusions historically encouraged and rewarded by the private sector.

Our three areas of inquiry—creativity, social well-being, and collaboration—create cultural feedback loops. All three inquiries arise from areas of research that show them to be measurable and predictive of outcomes in population health, economic development, community integration, labor productivity, and more.

In some ways, the Courageous Imagination framework is a cultural identity Rosetta Stone for company's to understand how to use research from neuroscience, psychology, health, arts and management literature to enhance investment strategies.

Our cultural identities are important because they inform how we make meaning and create value in our lives and in different situations. For example, Mark Zuckerberg's lived experience may cause him to ask one set of questions from a data set, but, what about the lived experience of a Black lesbian in Appalachia, or a single mother in rural Colorado who is Hispanic? From a scientific, mechanistic view, all three of these examples are similarly creating meaning and value in their lives. Their cultural identities, however, guide the context and convergent goal direction for what is most meaningful and valuable to each of them individually.

Moving beyond individuals, we must also consider the groups in which individuals work. The group-level is, perhaps, the most important focus area for research exploration of creativity and the future of work.

As part of a National Science Foundation-sponsored research lab in 2018, I assembled and led a team that started developing an analytics instrument called the Cultural Wellbeing Index. We theorized that, by measuring hope, trust, and belonging, we could forecast employee health, retention, engagement, and other key performance indicators critical to an organization's innovation capacity. Over the years and across sectors, it has proved to be true. Moreover, the specific combination of those three metrics has proven more predictive than any one metric alone.

Recently, with my primary research partner, Cameron Lister, we applied our cultural analytics research approach to assist the State of Colorado in developing a Small Business Resilience Index. During Covid, hope, trust, and belonging explained more variance in small business resilience in Colorado than any other variable, including access to capital. These are meaningful measures.

To clarify a common misconception, hope is not optimism. Optimism is the belief that things will work out in the future. Action on the part of the individual holding the belief is not required. Hope, on the other hand, is assessing the agency of the individual to act. Hopeful people take action to envision an uncertain future state, begin acquiring resources, and use those resources to create multiple pathways to that future uncertain goal. Hope is a powerful construct of personal agency and is teachable.

Trust. Most leaders talk about "building" trust. Well, that's not how trust works. Trust is an earned relationship. It can be very fragile. Trust is also not output. It's something in which you continually invest. Trustworthy relationships are the goal.

Belonging—or maybe even more importantly, mattering—is where I believe the most impactful opportunities for intervention reside. There are three levels of belonging inquiries to consider when designing interventions. They are the same three questions we all use to navigate when we walk into rooms where there are people we don't know: Am I safe? How am I connected to these people? In what ways is my future connected to this group's success?

How each of us answers these questions influences how much of ourselves—our creativity and social capital—we will give to any group effort. Measuring this multidimensional sense of internal belonging predicts a company's capacity to respond to its external environment.

In business, we often put innovation in one part of a company. Then, we take our culture change initiatives and put them in another part, like human resources. We most often think of innovation as a growth strategy requiring investment for a rate of return. We think of culture change programs—like diversity, equity, and inclusion—as cost centers with some vague public relations or risk-mitigating function.

However, when you look at the management research, both initiatives have around the same failure rate of around 60%. Why? Because they are different functions of the same idea. Innovation involves disruption, which invokes cultural change.

Cultural change cannot happen without innovation, so they are firmly connected. The cultural data analytics approach our team developed and validated inside a National Science Foundation-sponsored research lab begins establishing a quantitative data bridge between those two functions.

In the Imaginator Academy we expand on our original research on hope, trust, and belonging. The Courageous Imagination framework introduces metrics and data visualization dashboards related to creativity, curiosity, social well-being, compassion, awe, oppositional courage, and several other critical human experiences shown across research to enable people to work, learn, heal and explore together. With wonderful research partners, like Hannah Merseal, who is also presenting later today, our work expands the utility and deployment of the most critical creativity metrics in research. Bringing them into companies as actionable intelligence is the goal.

Collectively, this body of work holds significant promise as a set of quantifiable signal indicators of the cultural capacity of companies seeking to innovate. It all begins, though, with identity. Who we conceive ourselves to be—as a human being, a professional, a wife, a brother, a lover, an artist, a leader, and so on. The stories we tell about who we are matter because they provide the context for how each of us makes meaning in our personal and professional lives.

The final piece Imaginator Academy seeks to understand is how our work can shape society. Of course, how a for-profit Fortune 100 company innovates will look different than how a grassroots organization innovates. However, the mechanisms at play, and, perhaps even the goals, are controlled by the same thing: the desire for self-determination and freedom. Research demonstrates that autonomy has a multiplier effect for both wellbeing and creativity.

Regarding creativity research, Dr. Maggie Boden is a NorthStar for me. Her work outlines three types of creativity: exploratory, combinatory, and transformative. Lately, it has occurred to me that these three types of creativity also represent varying degrees of freedom in different executive leadership teams.

Exploratory creativity often occurs when leaders are in companies defined by a specific discipline. There's a gatekeeper who decides whether a novel idea has value or not. That's great if you're talking about a pharmacological intervention. In that case, I want somebody who understands the laws of chemistry and biology to quash an idea that might kill a person if ingested. However, as we move further into the socio-cultural parts of our lives, whose "value" should be the deciding factor? In these cases, historical gatekeepers may not add much value and not do much more than reinforcing their own historical power. One truism about power is that it reinforces itself.

Expanding further, Boden writes of combinatorial creativity. We take an idea from one discipline and put it together with an idea from another. We've achieved the first condition of creativity, novelty, but is the combination of ideas useful or valuable?

Maybe. Maybe not. Who should decide?

Finally, Boden points us to transformative creativity where a major shift occurs that fundamentally alters the way value is perceived. What would this look like in today's world? The iPhone is an example of such a shift, which has transformed how we understand "product" value making certain exploratory creativity questions less relevant. It also transformed our collective experience of how we "human" together.

In all three forms of creativity, context is important, and cultural changes often serve as the context. Culture is the context in which all three forms of creativity live.

Over these last two years in America, the cultural context implies that we have not just gone through COVID, but also a long overdue racial reckoning sparked by the murders of Breonna Taylor, George Floyd, and many others.

Globally, the cultural context implies generational value shifts. Gen Z, the very first generation ever to grow up in a digital world, are demonstrating an increasingly deep commitment to environmental, social, and economic justice. The oldest of Gen Z is also turning twenty-five this year. This generation, 20% of the global workforce by 2025, is calling for transformative thinking—not more gatekeepers.

The future of culture is being formed by shocks and shifts like these examples and many others. This brings us full circle and back to our cultural identities. In the opening, when I asked you to think about a person that was meaningful to you, my guess is that it was a personal relationship based on a part of your identity which you hold dear. It was specific to you. Though we all were sitting in the same room, we each had a radically different human experience considering how we each answered the question. This is why a "one size fits all model" can't deliver what's needed for cultural transformation in the future of work.

We've all seen the World Economic Forum and McKinsey & Company reports. The future of work will require a massive digital skills transformation and upskilling areas that are deeply human—cognitive, interpersonal, self-leadership, and so on. I believe that the arts and humanities must be central to our transdisciplinary development.

After all, the meaning-makers among us have roots stretching back to before our hunter-gatherer days. Why have we siloed and sidelined them so? Science is massively important. But, seeds turned in earth, even before we had words to name flowers.

Earlier today, we discussed how psychology recently started focusing on the vital role of creativity. We debated how the world doesn't wait for institutions to catch up. People have always been self-forming and self-organizing. Far from threatening, I suggest we reclaim our sense of wonder in what's possible, together. If we can put aside ego and defensive posturing, new options become visible. I humbly suggest that this is an important role for poetry. Language bigger than what science can hold. I offer this provocation from another of my poems: Only a poem can survive, intact and humble, she thrust into a tunnel of bluster and fury.

With that in mind, in the coming months, Imaginator Academy is launching the first-ever Workforce Census of Creativity & Belonging in America. An early-stage pilot to explore what I believe... namely that the great resignation shows Americans' new life as people of Courageous Imagination. A beginning of the next Enlightenment. Only this time, radically diverse. Many media outlets today declare that America's legendary brand of imagination capacity has declined. I don't think that's true at all. It just looks different today. I celebrate that! Further, it seems to me the most important question is what are people are running toward? Not, what are they running from? Imagination is happening right now. Today, the present is how we futureproof our world.

I'm a neurodiverse, blind-in-one-eye, queer person from a nine-generation family in the Appalachian Mountains. It is a place that is very, very poor, economically. It is also rich beyond belief, culturally. The courage and imagination in that little remote place are on par with Silicon Valley. Is it creating the economic impact of Silicon Valley? Absolutely not. But it is on par with the most exceptional human imagination, anywhere.

As much as any research, it's my lived experience that forms the roots of my work today. My work today is scientific but was not devised in a laboratory. Instead, its origin story is found in a community nonprofit led by artists called IDEAS xLab, which I co-founded with my husband, Josh Miller. We were quickly joined by other artists, like Hannah Drake.

Our original premise is as true today as it was at the beginning: stories are what change the world. In today's world, data makes those stories investable and scalable. No matter how you construct your identity - scientists, artists, business leader - ask yourself this questions. What would it mean to live the best story you can tell?

I'll close today with the words of James Baldwin, who wrote:

"The precise role of the artist, then, is to illuminate that darkness, blaze roads through that vast forest, so that we will not, in all our doing, lose sight of its purpose, which is, after all, to make the world a more human dwelling place."

10. Decide To Be Creative! An Exploration Of The Role Of Creative Self-Beliefs In Translating Creative Potential Into Creative Behavior

Izabela Lebuda[1,2], Aleksandra Zielińska[1], and Maciej Karwowski[1]
[1]Institute of Psychology, University of Wrocław, Poland
[2]Institute of Psychology, University of Graz, Austria

If you're reading this book, we think it's safe to assume that you find creativity to be an interesting topic, and an important one at that. Regardless of our perspective on creativity—whether we see it from the viewpoint of a parent, teacher, entrepreneur, artist, or scientist—we probably share the same goal: to encourage people to be more creative. As fans of the subject of creativity, we can quickly generate many different suggestions on how to achieve this. Let's try for the time being to look at the most obvious solution. Could it perhaps be enough to simply ask people to be creative?

Research on instructions' impact on the effectiveness of solving creative tasks allowed researchers to identify the "be creative effect" (e.g., Nusbaum et al., 2014). It has been shown that people who are instructed to "be creative" tend to come up with fewer, but more original, ideas than their counterparts who are asked to provide as many ideas as possible (a so-called "be fluent" instruction). Of course, it isn't easy to find unambiguous answers in scientific research. Many conditions also modify the regularity described above. For example, the "susceptibility" to instruction is much stronger among people characterized by a higher level of intelligence (Nusbaum et al., 2014). However, the fact that a "request" can modify the effects of creative thinking proves that we can effectively control, at least to some extent, our cognitive processes leading to new and valuable solutions. Contrary to the still-functioning lay belief that creativity is a "magical," "ephemeral" process, and that we are left at the mercy of the muse, we have the possibility of intentionally directing and modifying our thinking accordingly to the set goal (e.g., Benedek et al., 2014).

Excellent! So, we know how to make people more creative or, more precisely, make them think more creatively. However, it is worth remembering that creative thinking does not always result in creative action—one that we can actually observe and respond to. Many studies have shown that creative potential (including the ability to create new and valuable ideas) only partially explains how people undertake creative activities and translate them into successes (e.g., Lebuda et al., 2021). Thus, the question remains: What is necessary to transform this manageable potential into real action and observable behaviors that eventually may impact the reality around us?

More than two decades ago, one of the most prominent researchers in the field of creativity, Robert Sternberg (2002, 2003), indicated that creativity, as an activity that requires taking risks and simultaneously putting in a lot of conscious effort, is undertaken because of the so-called agentic decision. To make such a commitment, one needs to hold a set of appropriate beliefs about creativity. This reflection became the basis of a more formal proposal—the Creative Behavior as Agentic Action model (CBAA; Karwowski & Beghetto, 2019). This still dynamically developing theoretical conception (see Karwowski et al., 2019) posits that potential for creative thinking helps develop creative self-confidence. The belief that a task can be successfully performed motivates one to undertake this challenge in the first place. As a result, more creative people cope better with creative challenges and thus expect positive outcomes in subsequent, similar activities, in which they are also more willing to engage. Although the phrase "I can" sounds like a great marketing slogan, it is not enough to ensure actual creative activity. The second belief necessary for creative action, alongside creative confidence, is positive evaluation of creativity: recognizing creativity as an important value and an essential part of the self. Indeed, we can easily imagine, and perhaps even know, a person who can come up with astonishing ideas and who believes in their potential to resolve creative problems, but still does not take up this activity because they perceive it as fluff or a waste of time. Thus, it is assumed that transition from creative thinking to creative action is a decision-based process driven by creative confidence and positive valuation of creativity.

In a series of correlational and longitudinal studies, Karwowski and Beghetto (2019) showed that higher creative abilities translate into greater activity and achievement, but only among people who value creativity. Those for whom creativity is of little importance do not take up creative challenges, even if their potential is high. In an academic context, it was shown that self-confidence in creative tasks is associated with a higher level of self-regulatory skills and is positively associated with creative activities in the field of language learning and mathematics; interestingly, it is not related to achievements in these domains (Zielińska et al., 2021). What we think about our creative potential and how we value creativity is directly related to undertaking creative activities, but it does not guarantee success. Only persistent and deliberate practice in a chosen field leads to achievements. Thus, belief in our own creative abilities and positive creativity valuation is key to initiating a creative action and persevering in it, which in turn may lead to being noticed and appreciated by others (Lebuda et al., 2021).

As beliefs about creativity are known to play a critical role in the transition between ability and actual activity, the question arises as to whether we can influence how people perceive creativity. Following the classic Albert Bandura's research on self-efficacy (1997), there are four primary sources of these judgments. The first, as previously mentioned, is the history of personal successes. The second is an emotional experience; based on how we feel while performing certain activities, we continue with those that are both pleasant and result in long-term well-being, and withdraw from those that are a source of discomfort or long-term malaise. The next source of self-beliefs is verbal persuasion. Direct messages, especially from significant people, shape how we perceive ourselves and our abilities. Last, but not least, is vicarious learning, also known as observational learning. In this case, we acquire knowledge by observing other people, especially their rewards or punishments, so we learn from other people's mistakes (and successes).

These four mechanisms initially described in the context of general beliefs regarding our own agency also play a crucial role in shaping creative self-beliefs. Even elementary interventions can change our judgments about the nature of ability (Karwowski et al., 2020). In a simple experiment, the definition of creativity was manipulated. The first group of respondents got acquainted with the description of creativity, and were given examples of everyday creative activities, such as cooking, coming up with a new game, or decorating the apartment. The second group read the definition of creativity, which referred to outstanding creative achievements and figures such as Albert Einstein and Frida Khalo. It turned out that the group presented with the definition of everyday creativity believed in the possibility of developing and learning creativity more than those in the other group. On the contrary, the participants who read about eminent creators were more likely to agree that creativity is an innate talent that cannot be changed. Whether or not we believe a given ability can improve over time regulates how we behave. The mindset we adopt plays a critical role in the event of potential difficulties or failures. People inclined to believe that creativity cannot be developed tend to give up when faced with challenges (Beghetto & Dilley, 2016). Since they have not been able to complete a task successfully and it is not very likely to improve oneself in the future, there seems to be nothing else to do but quit.

The described research shows how "sensitive" to changes beliefs about creativity are. Even very subtle influences caused a significant shift in beliefs. The long-term intervention on self-beliefs had a similar effect (Zielińska et al., 2021). Participants in this study completed an online diary for 16 days, half of which were spent solving very simple tasks focused on building their creative confidence and appreciation for creativity. On the remaining days, participants were not presented with such tasks. The proposed creative challenges were simple and relatively undemanding: they did not require additional materials and took the respondents no longer than 10 minutes to complete. You can see examples of these tasks in Table 1.

Table 1. Example Tasks

Your task for the next day will be... vigilance! Throughout the day tomorrow (regardless of whether you will be at work, at the university, at home, or at a meeting), try to see as many things as possible that surprise you, seem unobvious, etc. These can be very different things and phenomena—related to nature, interpersonal contacts—anything. Try to notice and ask what others do not see.

Below are some memes that show things/solutions that are not currently available that could be both original and meaningful and make our lives easier or better... Look at them and try to come up with a few of your own ideas for such small creative solutions.

The task for tonight and tomorrow morning is... to watch ads! Take a look at what is being advertised and how and note those ads that are particularly surprising and original.

It was shown that on days when the respondents were externally motivated to pay attention to creativity, they declared that they were more creative and engaged more in everyday creative activities than on other days. It's important to note that this type of intervention was ineffective in domain-specific and more professionalized creativity. Considering the domain-general nature of the intervention, this result is not surprising. However, it is interesting to see which of the proposed tasks supporting creative self-beliefs worked most effectively. In another online diary study, which lasted for a month, participants approached two kinds of tasks. For half of the days, they completed tasks focused on supporting creative abilities, like divergent thinking. For another half of the study, the tasks were more motivation-oriented— aimed at supporting knowledge and interest in creativity, creative confidence beliefs, and positive creativity valuation. Examples of such tasks can be seen in Table 2.

Table 2. Example Tasks		
Abilities-Oriented	**Divergent Thinking**	There is a Ministry of Yoga in India. Try to come up with three additional, unusual—BUT USEFUL!— ministries that would be worth establishing in Poland.
Motivation-Oriented		Imagine this year you can choose a candidate for the Nobel Prize (in any field). Who would you pick? Give your answer tomorrow.
	Creative	Think about yourself and your qualities for a moment. Which of them could you develop to become an even more creative person than you already are? List these qualities and plan how to strengthen and develop them.
	Valuing Creativity	Over the course of today and tomorrow, try to generate some sensible reasons for being creative. What does this give us? What does it mean for ourselves and other people? Whether—and why! —it is worth developing your own and other people's creativity. Try to ask yourself this question in different situations—at home, work, in private and professional settings—at the university and outside, on the street and in the store.

It turned out that supporting creative self-beliefs translates into subjectively assessed creativity and everyday creative activity to a greater extent than supporting the ability to think creatively. While the results of this intervention were not very strong, it is worth highlighting that the participation in the study and performing the tasks also did not require much commitment. Therefore, it seems promising to incorporate the motivation-oriented challenges in traditional, more cognitively oriented creativity training, and to welcome them into our daily lives.

To conclude, we have control over our creative thinking, but an agentic decision is necessary to realize this creative potential. For this undoubtedly risky endeavor, we need to acknowledge two factors: an appreciation for creativity, and the belief that we can successfully solve tasks that require creativity. Importantly, both judgments can be effectively cultivated in an undemanding way. We hope that this short excerpt will help you make optimal decisions regarding your creativity.

Acknowledgement

Izabela Lebuda was supported by funding from the European Union's Horizon 2020 research and innovation program under the Marie Skłodowska-Curie grant agreement No 896518.

**Literature for this article can be found on Page 89

11. Rethinking Education With Ootiboo: Project-Based Curriculum With Creativity As A Vehicle

Kathleen Schroeter, CEO ootiboo GmbH, Vice-Chair VRBB

I always say I'm a human/nerd-interface, which comes from my background as part of the Fraunhofer Association for 13 years. I use that work experience now to endeavor in my new adventure of co-founding a company called Ootiboo to inspire creativity in children. In a nutshell: we use creativity as a vehicle to strengthen mental health and develop future skills in our children. We focus on two main objectives: Mental Health and so-called Future Skills. Why is that needed? 30% of people between the ages of 10 to 19 years old are diagnosed with a mental health disorder; anxiety and depression make up about 40% of these disorders. We have estimated that 45,800 teenagers commit suicide each year. The pandemic exacerbated these numbers.

Everything in the world is connected. I'm also a yoga teacher and a permaculture designer. Permaculture is mainly concerned with saving soil. At an event about soil, the Indian yoga guru and advocate of spirituality Sadhguru talked about the World Health Organization, stating that we are in a pandemic of mental health. Farmers, particularly those in the United States, are committing suicide at an exponential rate. The executive director of UNICEF has said: "When we ignore the mental health of children, we undercut their capacity to earn work, build meaningful relationships and contribute to the world."

This leads me to highlight the second focus in our work, the future skills. It's estimated that 65% of today's school children will work in professions that do not currently exist. We don't know what these jobs are. How do we prepare a skill set for that? When we look at how we are wired, humans have these common drives. It doesn't matter where you're born, or when you were born if you're a human being.

Your grandparents were driven by these impulses, and your grandchildren will follow suit. When we are in the process of developing something technological - something that we hope is innovative - if we don't understand these impulses and satisfy them, then we are creating a gadget, not an innovation.

Let's look again at how we are wired. Maslow's pyramid of needs may seem old-fashioned, but it's still quite relevant today. Each level is a base for the next level. When you look at the very basic needs of physiological and safety needs, the next level is the need for love and belonging. When we don't feel safe, we literally can't step to the next level of this pyramid, and we can't face the big problems of humanity.

When it comes to future skills, the World Economic Forum emphasized that resilience, stress tolerance and flexibility were high on the list of priorities. A study called "The future of work survey" shows some interesting figures and facts on jobs that will crop up by the year 2025. Approximately 85 million jobs may be displaced by the shift in the division of labor between humans and machines. On the flip side, 97 million jobs may emerge that are adapted to the new division of labor between humans, machines and algorithms. We may have to switch skill sets, but our education system is not prepared. We could close the skill gap, and we could add 11.5 trillion US dollars to the global GDP by 2028. We must find a way to build the business around our solution.

Ootiboo evolved from large-scale community projects between myself and my ex-colleague and good friend Angus. Angus already did large community art projects in the south of England. Outcomes showed how everything orbited around teamwork, inclusion and free expression. Failure is okay and there shouldn't be any pressure to perform. There is no right and wrong. There's no best mark. It's just asking you to contribute and be a part of it.

Let's consider these two examples from that earlier work from before we founded ootiboo.

About 50 minutes from London off the coast of Kent, there's a beautiful beach site that's much more affordable than London and still affords people a commute if they need to go into the office once or twice a week. A lot of creatives have been going there in the last couple of years, and Angus, our co-founder, also founded a group of creatives called the EASTCLIFF creatives. One of their projects involved celebrating the memorial of the end of the First World War. Keeping in mind that the poppy is the symbol of the end of the First World War, they decided to use the beach as their canvas and ended up painting 48,000 pebbles in memoriam, laying the stones out to create the shapes and colors of poppies! Around 2,000 people helped with this project, including teachers, students, parents, and even tourists.

People became very nurturing towards the concept, tidying up any stone that happened to get nudged out of place in its poppy shape and demanding respect for the installation. The pebbles were not only painted in red but also had some personal drawings on them. During one of the drawing workshops, one person drew a star of David next to a mosque on these pebbles. Older people explained to the kids the importance and significance of the poppies and what lay behind that symbol. It was truly a beautiful demonstration of inter-generational communication and engagement.

What is interesting about Kent, specifically Folkestone, is that this town is closest to the European mainland, and on a clear sky day, you can see France from the coast.

That's why it's important. This coastline was an important part of WWI. One lady living in Folkestone, who is the head of strategy at a book publisher called Farshore, recognized how engaging this project was and how the participants experienced a new sense of belonging in the community. After establishing a new logo and name around the notions of community and reading, she suggested a "paper beach," in which many of the same kids who took part in the poppy pebble project handed in an A4 page answering the simple question: Where does reading take me? The answers were then colored into a beach scene, and the resulting mosaic morphed beautifully into the entire beach. It was unveiled in a live stream, and the contribution was amazing.

These two examples showed that people can come together and share an experience of being part of a larger purpose. It created positive memories and associations, and with that, we have a context for data. They have a story to tell. What if we brought out something systematic in that, something that could always work? This sense of belonging and ownership of something with people who come from totally different backgrounds could be a constant thing in life.

That's how ootiboo came about. The company is still very young. We concentrate on kids aged five to 11, but we've found a lot of companies and potential partners saying we have huge problems finding new young talent. It's oftentimes hard to fill the jobs that we are offering, so we were asked to offer something for the teenagers, as well. Considering that we have creatives and teachers, we could also come up with something like a curriculum, which is where we are now. Interdisciplinarity is key.

Another notable project we did involved the famous duo Ant & Dec, who are very well known in the UK and are something of a national treasure there. These TV stars have won the BAFTA for 20 years running. They are part of Family TV program, which means they have a huge outreach. They recently rolled out their first kids' book called "Propa happy" to the market. All the profits from that book go to the NSPCC, which is the National Society for the Prevention of Cruelty to Children. We were asked to help them launch the book with some relevant activities, rather than just have a launch party and book signings. They wanted more engagement, and we were more than happy to oblige the request! As Farshore, with whom we already worked previously, was the publisher for that book, they understood the massive potential. We asked for entries worldwide for some inspiring poems, drawings, paintings, etc. around a new question: What makes you happy? This example goes way beyond a school project.

This doesn't suggest that school projects are overlooked, of course. For example, I have been an advocate for quite some time for putting an A into the STEM acronym, which would then stand for science, technology, engineering, arts and math. We work with Egmont magazines and visit schools to ask kids to create their own planet. They can do that with playdough, building blocks, or drawings. The planet could be anything; there is no framework, and they can do what they want. We just want to know the name of the planet and which creatures are on the planet. Currently, this project takes place in South England, but we're reaching out and want to expand beyond the UK borders.

We also want to go beyond the concept of "reading for pleasure". Allow me to exemplify this endeavor. A friend of mine from the STEAM world and a well-known cinematographer and director, Jannicke Mikkelsen lives in one the most northern settlements in the world, Svalbard, where the population is only about 2,500 and 3,000 polar bears. Normally on the globe that kids have as a toy at home, Svalbard doesn't show, as the needle that holds the globe together tends to cover it up. Therefore, I was surprised to find that at my nephew's school, a map included the island of Svalbard, so I sent a picture of this map to Jannicke. It's so far north that most people don't realize that people are living there and that there is a school. In that school, students speak more than 60 languages, including Thai and Filipino.

With sponsorship from Canon and having worked with David Attenborough underwater and doing a 3D shooting with the rock band Queen, we tried to imagine how we could incorporate her talent and skills in new ways. She is also one of the few females in this creative industry, so we are hitting a lot of birds with one stone with Jannicke as a representative.

She was part of the last expedition into the Svalbard area where the polar bears are because, in 2023, the government will close off the area there. People will only be able to access up to a certain length degree with a snowmobile or skis, which makes it very difficult to investigate the environment and explore the effects of climate change on that very fragile landscape. The expedition team had a 4G tower set up, and we were able to have a WiFi bridge down to their camp, so we decided to rethink climate education. As she was shooting something there, doing live streaming from anywhere in the world seemed quite ambitious and exciting. Then we decided to have a live streaming to those 60 countries that are represented in Svalbard so that the kids in Thailand could see what other kids from Thailand do up in the north and how they live.

In Svalbard, you're not allowed to go outside without a rifle because of the danger of happening upon polar bears. You also get frostbite if you don't have your gloves on for a certain number of minutes. Kids around the world could begin to understand how fragile the world up there is, and Jannicke explained precautions, protocols, and environmental changes.

We want to make it accessible for kids to understand what happens there, and we want to give the power to the kids, for them to have a window of opportunity to ask the right question for themselves, rather than prompting questions we consider important. Instead, we ask them to collaborate with us and use design thinking methods to make the topics and content more tangible. We're still searching for partners and have already talked with TV and film producers about the idea of a new science program with live transmission from Svalbard every week and anywhere in the world. We may also adapt to certain time zones. More importantly, we want the kids to be involved and engaged.

I'd like to conclude with one last idea before I finish. Together with Janet Crea from

Aarhus University, we want to rethink what libraries are for. What are they doing already? What if multimedia is much more present? Can we use those so-called Next-Gen Technologies and bring that all together? We believe that the added value comes with the convergence of all these technologies. We're talking with Ableton, the software and hardware music company, as well as some entities in Korea. We're considering how we can use AI to empower the public to use their creativity and engage in complex decisions around the future of our world. As a team, we came up with a clear vision, with entries from 500 students. They can use AI to create some pictures of how they envision the future and what it could look like. We are always on the lookout for new partners with an interdisciplinary approach. We believe that changing progress travels in waves, much like a virus. Let's be influencers for one another.

12. Creativity: What We Know (And What We Don't)

Hannah M. Merseal, MS, Graduate Student at the Cognitive Neuroscience of Creativity Lab at PennState University

As a PhD candidate at Pennsylvania State University and a member of Dr Roger Beaty's team at the Cognitive Neuroscience of Creativity Lab, I'd like to share some thoughts regarding what we know about creativity, as well as perhaps what we do not know. My research has two primary tracks. First, I focus on the cognitive neuroscience of music improvisation. I essentially study how improvisers store, reference, and use musical patterns to create amazing and creative music in real-time. I do this work using a combination of computational, behavioral and neural methods. My second track of research has more to do with how we, as creativity researchers, can apply our work towards the common good—whether that's building equity in historically oppressed communities, creating new public policies, or fostering creativity in environments like school and the workplace.

Let's delve a little bit more into the state of creativity research at large. First, I'd like to talk about our scientific understanding of what creativity is, and it turns out that there are a lot of answers to this question. Creativity covers a fairly wide umbrella of domains. While typically, many people think of creativity in an artistic context, it's also a critical element in the sciences, technology and innovation, as well as in problem-solving. Research groups like mine tend to think about creativity as a confluence of different ordinary cognitive processes that are all operating at their peak. This includes different types of memory, attention, controlled thinking, learning, as well as making associations between different ideas.

At the same time, our creative and innovative capacity has a lot to do with development, and individuals' understanding of creativity, as well as the types of creativity they engage with, are influenced by factors such as language, their education, the families they grew up with, as well as their cultural context. From this, it becomes clear to us that not only is creativity internally driven, but it is also heavily influenced by our environment, the problems we face, and the resources that we are afforded. This environment can be larger—like the country or the larger community that we belong to—but also in smaller environments, like the workplace and at home. In short, it's safe to say that creativity is complicated! Creativity requires so many things to go right. It involves so many moving parts, and there's no single, perfect definition, and yet, creativity is such a globally important concept that it behooves us as a species to try and understand it the best that we can.

Not only is creativity broad, but it is also ubiquitous. Creativity has been the driving force behind every human innovation and every problem that we have solved as a species. Creativity is the most vital human trait: it isn't even replicable by artificial intelligence. With that being said, creativity researchers face the unique burden of communicating the findings of our work to the world in a way that is both understandable and actionable.

The process by which scientists conduct and communicate their research is so opaque and inaccessible at times that it often feels like we are shouting our findings into the void of an echoing canyon, praying that it reaches the other side. A 2021 study by Benedek and some illustrious colleagues sought to find out exactly how much of our shouting is making it to that other side. Despite decades of research aiming to demystify creativity, there are many popular beliefs out there that are not supported by scientific evidence. Many of these myths arrive from anecdotal evidence or warped interpretations of scientific findings. Over a sample spanning six countries and over 1,200 participants, the authors assessed public approval of several popularly held beliefs about creativity that are incorrect based on the scientific evidence we have available. They also included some findings, which we think are true, which means that they are consistently found in the creativity literature. I will show you some of these statements now, and we can play a little game of True or False.

First, it is false that **children are more creative than adults.** This is not a finding that has consistently been found in the literature (Torrance, 2008).

The first idea someone has is often not the best one. True. Oftentimes, we see that as we go through a process of idea generation, our ideas increase in novelty and usefulness (Beaty & Silvia, 2012).

Next, **creative people are usually more intelligent.** True. Pretty consistently, we find high correlations between creativity and intelligence (Jauk et al., 2013).

Creative ideas are naturally a good thing. Ask any serial killer, and we can deduce that's a false one (Cropley et al., 2010).

People who have more creative ideas are under the influence of alcohol or marijuana. False. This is not a very consistent finding in the literature (Norlander, 1999).

A man's creativity increases his attractiveness to potential partners. True (Kaufman et al., 2016).

Creative thinking mostly happens in the right hemisphere of the brain. Absolutely, categorically false—if you come out with nothing else from these chapters, rest assured that you use your whole brain, all the time (Abraham, 2018).

Across all six countries, the authors found these beliefs to be fairly widespread across both the creativity myths and the facts presented. Myths were approved on average by 50% of people, with a range between 20% believing that people have a certain amount of creativity and cannot do much to change it, and 80% of people believing that brainstorming in a group generates more ideas than if people were thinking by themselves, which is again, not a consistent finding in the literature. Belief in these myths was related to having fewer years of education, endorsement of popular neuroscience myths, endorsement of creativity facts, and references to popular media. They are higher on neuroticism, conscientiousness, authoritarianism, belief in the paranormal, and lower creative self-identity.

If one thing is clear to us from this study, it is that right now, we are not effectively communicating creativity research to the public. This might be for many reasons: the general distrust and misunderstanding of the scientific process, the fact that most peer-reviewed journal articles are not free to read for the public, miscommunications of scientific findings by popular media, or even the heavy jargon that we use to communicate our findings.

But why does it matter if our work makes it across the chasm? It matters because we live in a rapidly changing technological landscape, in which between 3 to 14% of jobs are expected to become automated by the year 2030. This is a shift that has only accelerated in the context of the COVID-19 pandemic. Creativity is among the most valuable attributes that individuals, businesses and even nations can have today. It remains the human ability least achievable by artificial intelligence. Translating our work to the public, and the world outside of the ivory tower of academia in meaningful ways has never been more important. In light of this, we have the responsibility of taking the necessary steps to improve accessibility and the communal understanding of creativity and of closing that gap.

I would now like to talk a bit about a science communication project I undertook with the Sonophilia Foundation after receiving their Outstanding Young Scientist Award in Creativity Research award. This project is called the Creativity Factbook, which aims to communicate the current state of the field in creativity research to a non-researcher audience. We conducted a lengthy literature review of the field and selected 99 "facts", or findings that have consistently emerged in the past half-century of creativity research. We only considered findings that came from high-quality empirical studies or meta-analyses that have been published in peer-reviewed journals. For each fact, we wrote up a bite-sized, easy-to-understand version of the fact alongside a slightly longer explanation referring to complementary sources. The curation team on this project consisted of Seda, Theo Edmonds and myself, as

we searched for facts over an active period of about three months last year. We had some fantastic and eye-opening conversations about creativity in our morning meetings. Broadly, the facts we found fell into five categories. The first was creativity's relationship with mental, social, and physical well-being. The second category was the connection between creativity, culture and environment. The third category encompassed findings about how we foster and improve creativity in education and at work. Next, we found articles in the two bins that I work with the most, which are the cognitive mechanisms, as well as the neural mechanisms, underlying creativity. I will give an idea of some of the kinds of facts we found, citing one representative fact from each area.

First, in terms of well-being, **engaging in creativity is generally related to feeling happier and more active.** In a meta-analysis of over 100 studies, Baas and colleagues (2008) found that creativity is enhanced by being in a positive mood rather than a negative one.

In our category of culture and creativity, Fürst & Grin (2021) found that **speaking a second language was positively related to almost all indicators of creativity** such as achievements, activities and performance on creative tasks.

For our category on fostering and improving creativity, Shin & Zhou (2012) found that teams with **creative leaders are themselves more creative.**

Next, our neuroscientific understanding of creativity shows that **creativity is a whole brain process** (Beaty et al., 2018). More creative individuals have higher connectivity between regions in the default network, which is associated with flexible thinking, and the executive control network, which is a source associated with more controlled and deliberate thinking.

Several papers by Yoed Kenett and colleagues have found that the overall cognitive process of creativity is highly associative, and **people who can combine distantly related or unrelated concepts are generally more creative** (Kenett & Faust, 2019).

Throughout this project, it became very clear to us that there are many things that we do know pretty concretely about creativity. At the same time, however, there is a much larger pool of information that we do not know, which readers may have already garnered. Unfortunately, many of these items I see as obstacles to doing meaningful and applied work that helps real people. Creativity research to date has been very Western, very white, educated, industrialized, rich and democratic (or WEIRD, to put it simply as an acronym). This is a broader problem in social science in general, but it's clear from the existing research that while we have a very good understanding of creativity in white university undergraduates in Europe or the US, we know very little about creativity in anyone else. This matters because the interaction between environment and cognition is so important for creativity. Individuals with lower socioeconomic status, individuals in different parts of the world, or individuals who have faced significantly different obstacles in their lives from those that we typically see are probably going to have different motivations for creativity, and they're going to have different opportunities to develop creative thinking skills.

Here we see a barrier between the worlds of cognitive and social science: cognitive neuroscientists frequently ignore the cultural contexts in which creative cognition occurs, and organizations who are out trying to boost creativity in the general public are not operating with an understanding of how learning and memory in the brain operate during creativity. This is a major problem for us when we try to move our research out of the lab and into the real world.

With all this in mind, I have some action items for the research community, for leaders in different organizational contexts who would like to improve creativity, and for people who want to be more creative in general. First, for the scientific community, we must make our work accessible and understandable to the public. As it stands, our research is often hidden from ordinary people behind steep paywalls, and for those who can afford to jump past them, our writing is so opaque that people outside of academia cannot understand what we're doing, and why it's important. We need to write better, and then we need to make that writing openly available to anyone who wants to see it. In addition to this, we need to leave the ivory tower sometimes and work with the community, both to communicate our research and to gain a better understanding of what our community needs us to research. Along those same lines, we need to conduct our research using samples that are reflective of the real world in which creativity occurs. With technology where it is today, it has never been easier to collect careful and targeted samples from around the world which reflect the underlying demographics of the environment. Further, we need to break down the wall between the worlds of cognitive and social science. We know that creativity results from interactions between the internal individual and their external environment. Our models, our samples, and our conclusions need to reflect this truth.

For leaders around the world—whether you lead a small team or a large organization, the scientific community needs you. Scientists navigate an unsustainable number of obstacles to this work. We are underfunded, and under-resourced and frequently do not have access to research participants who don't attend our immediate universities. I would ask that you have conversations with scientists: find out what their work is, explore what they need to do that will help improve creativity in your organizations and communities, listen to our findings, and then use our research to inform your policies and your guidelines.

For people who would just like to be more creative, the first step is to be open to learning. If you're reading this, you've become privy to some great thoughts about having healthy skepticism and asking where data come from, and how experiments are designed to create that data. There is a wide world of research out there and it can be overwhelming, but if you see a piece of research on Facebook or Twitter, take the extra steps to investigate where it came from. Was it from a trusted source? Was it from a peer-reviewed experiment? Ask these questions before sharing information or taking it to heart. This is a critical step in dispelling myths about creativity and science at large.

To this last point, I would like to share an upcoming special issue of Translational Issues in Psychological Science, on which Roger Beaty was the guest editor and I was an associate editor (see Merseal et al., 2022). This ended up being a great collection of articles bringing creativity out of the lab and into the real world. To those who worked on the Factbook, the Sonophilia Foundation, the Cognitive Neuroscience of Creativity Lab at Penn State, the authors on the Benedek et al. paper, and all of the authors who we cited in the Factbook, thank you all.

Q&A

Q: I have a question from the musician and design thinking community. Design thinking has changed since Tim Brown, at least partly. I think it's brilliant and fascinating what you do. As a musician, when I do innovation work, I use metaphors of music a lot, as if it's a symphony of innovation. I often compare design thinking. This innovative process is improvising on stage, which is what jazz musicians do. So I have a very particular question: why do you study musical improvisation?

Hannah: I'm also a musician! I have played the clarinet for almost my entire life, and I had a semi-popular jazz and funk band when I was an undergraduate. Jazz is very near and dear to my heart, and I'm just fascinated by it. The sheer amount of cognitive obstacles that a jazz musician has to overcome to improvise in real-time is amazing and, fortunately for me, perhaps understudied. It's just such a delightful area of research.

Q: I'm in a very different line. I teach fiction and nonfiction writing. But your presentation spoke to me and in fact, I discuss some of the ideas in class, which is an association of different kinds of ideas. I teach juniors and sophomores. What do you do to discuss or explore the research impact of these youngsters who are doing a ton of social media (like TikTok) and the impact of that on creativity? Any thoughts on that?

Hannah: I think that this is a great example of using our culture to guide our research questions. To my knowledge, there hasn't been that much done looking at social media use and even TikTok in particular, which I don't think has been a big topic of study. This is creative, but it's also taking up a lot of attention and cognitive resources in our youth. I think that, in collaboration with ootiboo, and other organizations, we are incorporating research elements into this work. This is another way of getting these very targeted samples, while also participating in life-changing work when we can do this research with real people from very diverse backgrounds, while they engage in this cool program
.

Q: I was wondering if you could talk about the factbook and the process you're using for creating the accessible language around each area that you're going to put forward.

Hannah: We had a lot of conversations where we threw back and forth topics and I would maybe try to explain a paper, and Seda was great about telling me, "That makes no sense to me, break that down a little bit further". So that was a major learning process for me. I think as we've combed through a lot of this material, it's gone through multiple people, and if it doesn't make sense, someone's going to say that.

Q: We've got design thinking where we experience design, and we could say that being human-centered when you're prototyping something means you either co-create it with the audience or prototype or take it to the audience to iterate from them directly. Depending on who the fact is focused on, I would suggest that they're the people to check the accessibility of language. I've had projects where we go to the community and either they directly co-create with us, or we test iterate with them also to ensure the authenticity of voice if they're the ones we want to adopt and engage with it.

Hannah: Yes, I believe that testing this on real people before the general public is in the plan.

***Literature for this article can be found on Page 90-91**

13. Knowledge and Creativity

Dr. Yoed Kenett, Director of the Cognitive Complexity Lab, the Faculty of Data and Decision Sciences, Technion - Israel Institute of Technology

What is the role of knowledge in creativity and how can we potentially study it? Knowledge is a building block of creativity and the desired outcome of a lot of our processes, such as learning, education, and development. One common saying that we hear a lot is that knowledge is key. One may ask, however, a key for what? How does that correspond to evidence that expertise—more knowledge—narrows our creativity? After all, the more we learn about something, potentially, the more we're fixated on it. So, what is the role of knowledge in creativity? I am particularly interested in understanding how we can study its costs and benefits.

Highly embedded in theories on the creative process is the notion that we are moving away from prototypicality; as we try to come up with something novel or unique or uncommon, we try to move away from the most common response. In a sense, we do so by searching our memory and trying to move further and further away. What does that mean? How can we measure this process that is inherent and goes back to the early days of theories on creativity in the first half of the 20th century? To be able to do this process, we must make two very strong assumptions. The first assumption is that there is a space of knowledge that we are searching through, like the internet, for example. This requires us to assume that there is an abstract level of the mental representations of knowledge and that there is some order to it or some guiding principles that connect ideas. The second aspect is that there is a search process that we use to search through that space. One might ask: Can we study these principles? Do they correspond to how our cognitive system works and the neural substrates that realize these two types of assumptions that we're making? We can now, more easily than ever, study these concepts directly through computational tools that come from natural language processing and graph theory network science.

Network Science is a multidisciplinary field that has sprung from a branch of mathematics called graph theory. It has also been highly developed by other adjacent fields such as physics, statistics, computer science and social psychology. Over the past two decades, it has cut across all fields of science and has been used to study complex systems. It offers formal mathematical ways to represent complex systems, such as social structure, transportation routes, cognitive systems, or the brain. The use of network science tools to study the brain has revolutionized how we are now understanding brain structure and function.

In the early days of cognitive theory on memory and language, a lot of network terminology was used. Specifically, the seminal paper by Collins and Loftus (1975), argued that semantic memory is organized as a network, a structure that constrains spreading activation processes over this cognitive complex system. Much of my research uses very simple psycholinguistic tasks like free associations (what do you think of when you see an object) or semantic fluency (generate all the animals that you can think of in a minute) to represent empirically derived networks of groups or individuals, and study the properties of these structures, spaces, maps, networks, with behavior, creativity, intelligence, openness to experience, aesthetics, etc. This work is summarized in a paper I published titled "A semantic network cartography of the creative mind" (Kenett & Faust, 2019). I use these network tools to map different knowledge systems, different memory networks, or structures that vary across individuals and groups in relation to different complex behaviors.

A lot of my work centers around young adults, meaning students but has recently extended to young children and older adults. Once we can map out these memory, language, or knowledge systems, then we can move forward to more exciting types of questions about dynamics. I study two different types of cognitive dynamics: The first focuses on how we search through memory, how creative searches differentiate between non-creative searches, and how information retrieval systems mimic how we think and search our memory. The second type of dynamics is about how these systems change with time, that is typical aging as we move from childhood to adulthood. How does semantic memory change, and can we use these understandings to understand what predicts successful learning? What happens when we age in our memory system? In addition, we can also ask these questions in clinical populations, for instance, what happens when our memory system starts to break down? What is the difference in this sense between cases of schizophrenia and autism? These computational tools allow us to ask many, many questions that remain open. This is a fairly new line of research and the application of these tools to study what we call cognitive networks, or cognitive network science is very, very young, as very few people conduct this type of research at present.

The main line of my research during the past few years has been to look at the semantic memory structures or networks of groups. Specifically, we started with the associative theory of creativity, which proposes that higher creative individuals differ from lower creative individuals by something that has to do with their memory structure. We had two groups of highly creative individuals and low creative individuals generate free associations to 96 Cue words (the four most prototypical exemplars of 24 different categories). Using the free association responses at the group level, we estimated the organization of these cues in a theoretical conceptual space. What we found was that the semantic structure of the conceptual knowledge base of the less creative individuals in creativity was more spread out compared to the highly creative individuals. It was also more compartmentalized and broke apart into smaller sub-clusters or communities.

Finally, in this network, there were also fewer connections between concepts. We interpreted these findings in support of the associative theory of creativity, and found that such a spread-out organized semantic memory network of the less creative individuals inhibits the spreading of activation throughout the network, thus inhibiting the ability to generate remote, original, creative ideas. Thus, higher creative individuals have a semantic memory network structure where concepts are closer together and less organized. We argue that this type of structure where everything's closer and less organized facilitates a wider, broader and deeper search into memory, which is a lot of what we think about creativity - creating new client connections, recombinations, and the ability to connect remote ideas. We now have ways to formalize these ideas.

In other studies, we have shown how this structure enhances flexibility, as semantic memory structure that is more condensed and less organized is more flexible. Creativity varies across individuals, which led me and Dr. Mathias Benedek to develop a method to estimate or represent the memory structures of individuals. Using this approach, we replicated our group-based results, showing that similar individual-based differences in semantic memory networks relate to individual differences in creative thinking. These individual-based semantic memory network results, concerning creativity, have now been replicated in German, Chinese, and French, thus demonstrating the validity and robustness of this method. We now have mathematical variables to start defining objective measures and properties of what is the role of knowledge in creativity.

After establishing the feasibility of these tools to study creativity in young adults, we can move forward and ask these questions about children. One of our studies that were recently published was conducted in Switzerland—in collaboration with Dr. Roger Beaty—where the lead researcher in this project was interested in the effect of the environment on child development, especially of non-traditional schooling systems compared to traditional schooling systems. Thus, we estimated the semantic memory structures in children that go to a Montessori, a non-traditional schooling system, compared to children who go to traditional schooling systems. What we found was that children in the Montessori school system have a more flexible memory structure, mimicking what we find in young adults. In addition, the children in the Montessori School perform better on creativity assessment. The environment has an impact on how our memory systems mature. We can now start asking questions about the effect of the environment and the development of knowledge through these mathematical tools.

We can use these tools to focus on the other end of the lifespan – older adults. Over the past few years, I have been collaborating with Dr. Roger Beaty and Dr. Michelle Diaz, looking at the semantic memory structure of young adults versus older adults. We represent the semantic memory structure of young adults compared to older adults across three different samples. We found that the memory structures of older people are more organized, and thus more structured. Our findings are consistent with other Aging Network studies that show that as we age, our memory structure becomes more segregated, more separated and more organized. Perhaps this is because as we acquire more knowledge, we are better at differentiating across concepts. We need a communication system that allows for quick retrieval of information comprehension and production, but there is a cost. We also found that the memory structures of older people are less flexible and more fragile. As we age, we learn more information, but that has a cost on novelty and flexibility. Taken together, we can use these tools to assess this process and potentially ask how we can start impacting it to maintain the balance between structure and flexibility.

Jumping over to another very exciting project that is in the works in collaboration with Dr. Emmanuel Volle, where we are studying the effects of restructuring. Once we have the tools to represent memory systems in people, we can start studying how they change. We give our participants a riddle to solve. Participants are required to solve this problem in ten minutes. Before and after attempting to solve this riddle, we have them do a task that allows us to represent individual-based semantic memory networks, where they see pairs of words that are either related to the solution or not related to the solution of the problem. We compare the post-network with the pre-network for people that are successful vs. unsuccessful in solving, and we examine if there are any differences. According to theory and creativity on insight and problem solving, there is memory restructuring. What we find is the local effects of a successful solution, at the post-estimated memory structure. This suggests that for people who successfully solve this riddle, their post-estimated memory structure and the connections between words that are relevant to the solution are stronger.

Knowledge is facts that we learn, that we find, that we invent. Our experience shapes the connection between these concepts as we move forward across contexts, ages, individual differences, and learning opportunities. Creativity is potentially related to different connections, different connectivity patterns, and different types of memory organization. Now that we have the mathematical tools to study these differences, we can move towards investigating different types of questions in different types of populations, both in the lab and outside of the lab. Indeed, knowledge is key.

****Literature for this article can be found on Page 91

14. Exploring Creativity's Role In The Sustainable Development Goals

Discussants: **Marc Stickler, Photographer, Leica Ambassador and UN Changemaker & Faye Hobson, Program Director at The Salzburg Global Seminar,** Moderator: **Seda Röder, Founder of The Sonophilia Foundation**

When the topic of creativity comes up in conversation, it often brings real-world problems and questions about what it would take to bring about potential solutions. In 2015, the United Nations assembly published the Sustainable Development Goals, consisting of 17 objectives encompassing 169 targets for a more sustainable and collaborative future, to be revisited in 2030. Education, innovation, health, poverty, and climate action are just a few of the highlighted topics.

But what about creativity – nowhere in the document does the word 'creativity' even arise. Reflecting on these noble goals is no small matter, especially when we don't first consider how tasks of this magnitude can be achieved without fostering creativity. This is precisely what the Sonophilia Foundation set out to do in the panel discussion titled Creativity, Global Collaboration, and SDGs, which took place as part of their first-ever Cross-Atlantic Creativity Congress (CACC).

Acting as a mediator for the panel was Seda Röder, founder of The Sonophilia Foundation. The panelists, Marc Stickler, a Leica global ambassador and wildlife photographer, and Faye Hobson, program director at Salzburg Global Seminar, embarked on a roller coaster of a discussion on global creative collaborations and solutions for the world's greatest issues.

The problems set out in the SDGs are typically defined by institutions, which begs the question of how we are supposed to tackle them if real people on the field have such minimal influence in the process. Marc suggested we bring together many existing NGOs with a common goal to help bring about real and lasting change.

"We have to give back the power to the native communities," he began. "We have to encourage [and] empower them through education... We have to look at the people and the children first, and tackle the grand challenges face-on with all institutions, and there are so many NGOs out there."

Faye, for her part, has witnessed numerous collaborations and friendships struck in her work with Salzburg Global Seminar. As an international, nonprofit and strategic convening organization, many joint projects have been inspired by the valuable time spent and dialogue shared during any one of their organized programs. In reiterating the need to give the power back to indigenous communities, she believes a collaborative cross-sectoral systems approach is needed, one which takes into account all the inherent challenges.

"We need to rethink our relationship with the world and the planet," she said. "We use the sustainable development goals as a conceptual framework against which to map our work, and I know many of our arts and culture practitioners were involved in advocacy for culture being a goal within itself and the protection and preservation of culture being a goal within itself, and that didn't happen. That's indicative of why [I'm interested in] creativity because it's often not recognized as a powerful tool."

Bouncing ideas and topics off one another, the two panelists highlighted some of the most creative approaches to problem-solving that they've come across. Marc was particularly impressed with and inspired by the resilience of people – especially children – in underprivileged areas, where they seem to have the unique ability to build tools out of virtually anything. He drew on some experiences he'd had with handicapped children in the Tanzanian city of Arusha, in which one young boy born without arms used his feet to do everyday tasks, like writing with a pencil.

"When we can do everything and combust all obstacles in life, there is no boundary for us. The only stop is the imagination," Marc noted.

In the creative realm, making things happen under such rigid constraints can feel like both a blessing and a curse; one must come up with something out of nothing. This notion of using resources to their utmost capacity out of pure necessity led Faye to describe her involvement with community arts projects that focus on cultural innovation and social change.

"We recently launched a program," she said, "which is for education policymakers from around the world, supported by the Lego Foundation. It's specifically about bringing a breadth of skills-oriented reform into education systems around the world, with creativity being a key part of that. It's [heartening] to see that there is buy-in in certain parts of the world, both global north and global south about the need for creativity and that there are moves to start that."

At this point in the discussion, the topic of global collaboration came up, particularly regarding the idea of helping education professionals understand and consciously nurture different types of creative learning. This prompted participants to consider strategies that could help people work together and create trust in a way that would bring collaborations back to the field. Faye explained how Salzburg Global Seminar's programs often frame it from a research policy perspective.

"We try to bridge divides as people join a program, and we often ask, 'Who do you not know how to talk to?' to help people think about that. There are many toolkits and different approaches to collaboration and how to do that effectively. In an international context is being aware of the power dynamics inherent within that and what you're bringing into that space and what others may be bringing into it. Being cognizant of that, I think, is a really good place to start in international or intercultural collaboration."

Marc believes collaboration is the key to everything, and that to work together effectively, it's important to leave one's ego behind because personal gain has no place in a true collaboration. Common goals breed new beginnings, even if everyone wants to use their own tools or methods to reach the same end. He explained what it takes from a photography point of view.

"Just by working together, you leave the fight for resources [behind]... We are there to tell the same story after all, and that's what I tell other photographers. Even if there are other wildlife photographers, you have a beautiful picture but let's communicate because it's going in the same direction."

When the floor was opened to the audience to contribute, one participant posed an interesting question: What is a story we're all participating in, even though we know it's not true? This stimulated some fascinating responses, such as the concepts of economy, education, and religion. Another person underlined the necessity of giving and receiving feedback because this allows for more open communication. In short, critique is the essence of success in any collaborative endeavor.

Tying it back to the SDGs, one audience member wondered which would take the greatest priority. Although Marc was unable to choose just one, Faye said she would select Goal Four, which is quality education, because it seems to be where a lot of the problems start.

"If you look at planet relationships to each other through a social justice or a gender equity lens in terms of girls and women understanding their place in the world, I think all of that is rooted back to education systems. Suppose we can ensure quality education, which would mean equitable education and access to education all around the world. In that case, I think everything else should cascade from that in the longer term. Creativity-oriented education as well. That's very, very important."

The discussion was then steered in the direction of innovation within public governance and regulations in relation to the SDGs, with one person suggesting the governmental system itself is in dire need of creative solutions, as it is flawed beyond what many people comprehend. They argued that "we hold the power to reelect our government, but... you need top-down changes besides the bottom-up changes."

Seda brought the discussion to a close by making a statement about the SDG agenda, saying that global efforts are not being made readily available to the general public in a way that is easily understandable and that a more pragmatic approach is needed to change the world for the better.

"It's all on the paper or websites, but nobody knows what's happening unless they're already aware," she concluded. "As a result, the documents and the information are not getting to the people in the communities who actually can do something and change their behavior and change how they reelect their politicians... As long as it doesn't touch us and we're comfortable about that, not much changes... The politicians are the ones who can make the policies and who are responsible for taking action in this because many people just don't immediately see the effects of their behavior."

15. Deconstructing The Links Between Creativity, Entrepreneurship, And Technology*

Discussants: **Eva Wimmers, Investor, CEO and Founder of Geistesblizz & Peter Bruck, Director of the International Center for New Media,** Moderator: **Matthias Röder, Co-founder of the Sonophilia Foundation and CEO of the Karajan Institute**

*This panel discussion was brought on stage in cooperation with Innovation Salzburg GmbH & Interreg Crossinno Project.

"The mind is a terrible thing to waste." This slogan has never rung more true than it does now. Creativity is not a skill pegged only for a select few, nor is it a concept exclusive to the arts and humanities. The first-ever Cross-Atlantic Creativity Congress (CACC), organized by The Sonophilia Foundation, saw cutting-edge scientists, innovators, and decision-makers from diverse backgrounds exploring how to bridge the worlds of research, culture, business, arts, education, and society through the lens of creative thinking.

During the panel discussion titled Creativity, Technology and Entrepreneurship, the CEO and chief researcher of the Research Studios Austria Forschungsgesellschaft mbH Peter Bruck, and the CEO and founder of Geistesblizz GmbH Eva Wimmers, highlighted the joys and perils of creativity in the research and business world. With Sonophilia Foundation co-founder Matthias Röder as mediator, a lively and thought-provoking dialogue ensued on the role of creativity and how to boost it in everyday business situations.

As Chairman of the Board of Directors of The World summit Awards, an awards system selecting and promoting local digital innovation to improve society, Peter underlined the importance of understanding what motivates people. He made a distinction between art-based creativity and design-based creativity in terms of context but acknowledged that creativity must oftentimes come about by refusing to accept the conditions under which we live.

"It has very much to do with having different kinds of conversations and different kinds of formats of interaction," Peter began. "One of the things which troubles me when people talk about creativity is that it's so individualized... We all live in discourse. Discourse is before us, after us, and in between us, and it's the same thing with creativity. We are all creative together."
Eva supplemented these comments with some insight of her own, drawing on her

experience as an entrepreneur and top manager for various IT sector companies concerned with information, technology, and communications, such as Deutsche Telekom, Huawei, and Native Waves. Being a group thinker and taking initiative from her leadership structure, Eva believes inspiration can happen anytime, anywhere, and that putting the teams and employees at the heart of the strategy is when new and exciting things happen. She explained precisely how creativity in teams can come about and how big companies can be transformed into creative companies.

"It's a lot about bringing people into dialogue first, sharing what you're planning to do, that you're serious about it, and creating an environment where people dare to speak up because otherwise, it doesn't work," she said. "There are different ways of innovation and creativity. For a company, innovation is the output of creativity – we're looking for innovation that pays in the end. An idea that pays is the definition of innovation or creativity within the context of business. To be commercially successful in the future, growth alone is not sufficient anymore; it's all about sustainability - for people, the planet, and the company."

The two panelists then delved into the importance of dialogue and the issue of time necessary to hone and develop our creativity. Peter, for his part, reflected that time varies among cultures and is dependent on flexible and cohesive team building, rather than authoritarian, hierarchical structures.

"When time is alive, time flies, it's just very, very relative," he said. "I've not worked with a startup company which was able to stick with its original idea with each original thing. In the end, you come up with something similar to what you started with, which is very much related to how well you develop your skills over time, overcoming resistance, and that's the key issue. How do you pace yourself in that regard?"

Eva, on the other hand, called for patience in all aspects, from goal-setting to defining a specific problem or target. Executives must focus on taking time from the beginning to connect with the people, bring them into dialogue, and align the story of where the company wants to go and why, in addition to the KPIs and savings targets. Although she believes in quantifying the new route and vision, aligning people on the purpose, strategy, and the way to go and why is critical to mobilize energies within the organization. Without these components, Eva said a company can't hope to mobilize the workforce to grow.

"I know there's a lot of debate about [setting targets], whether they hinder the success of a company or not, but what do you want to do? Are you growing in this direction? What's your strategy to go there? Why do you need to change? Either you need a very strong prospect with a very strong target, or ideally, you have a burning platform for people to change. If you don't invest this time, it will take you forever, and I think this is one of the biggest misconceptions and transformations in companies."
From there, Matthias discussed technology and whether it helps us or distracts us from embracing our creative selves. This prompted a civil debate between the

panelists, with the two camps respectfully disagreeing on an empirical sociological level. Peter advocated for finding the context of how the technology is being used, emphasizing how every technology or intervention brings with it unintended consequences.

"Thirty years later, we look at the internet and we don't see it as a blessing, but a lot of people talk about it as a curse. Therefore, it's very, very clear that we can never say that technology is one or the other. It's always in the context," Peter said. "If you create a particular kind of context for seeing how digital creativity is used worldwide, to achieve SDGs, how we can use the technologies of the information society to create a knowledge society, then you are [embarking on] a path of mutual learning, which is incredible."

Eva countered by saying that technology often helps and supports unless it is being manipulatively or criminally misused or outright rejected. She believes the Digital Age is here to stay and we can only go forwards, not backwards, and embrace the technological advantages to best use.

"[When it comes to] creativity and global collaboration and coming together," she said, "if you had no technology, you would only know what your neighbor in your village does; you couldn't travel far enough to see something else... In essence, technology is a bridge between those people who refuse or who are not so literate in technology, or who are perhaps scared of technology... You can use technology to bring it towards people and to be more intuitive."

Weaved throughout the threads of this discussion was the question of highly localized, individualized creativity that comes from the top-down systems developed by multinational companies. Matthias pondered how to distinguish the directions of our creativity, as well as how individual and group creativity are connected, particularly when working creatively with technology.

In response, Eva cited the new parameters coming into play after two years of the COVID-19 pandemic, and now the war in Ukraine, saying: "We will have to rethink how 'New Work' aligns with 'New Living' in a more sustainable way... Through the pressures, as well as the mental health issues around the pandemic and the war and new lifestyle expectations, people refuse to get on the hamster wheel we created. Many who have never spoken of creativity simply aren't capable at this moment unless we support them. This may seem counterintuitive in our corporate minds, that when people stop performing or wanting to perform that we would support them, but if we want to come back and perform in our companies and the economy, we must understand that support and more creative ways are needed."

The audience was invited to contribute their thoughts on the subject. One attendee suggested that we use creativity to reduce the carbon footprint of a company, citing a bottom-up solution as opposed to a top-down one to create incentives among employees. Another participant said we must choose to use technologies to enhance our creativity rather than get sidetracked by them. They compared our preoccupation with technology to the Greek philosopher Socrates' belief that true dialogue and idea generation should occur physically, that storytelling and the need for connection, meaning, purpose, and unity are at the core of us as a species and that creativity is inherent in us.

Eva responded by reinforcing that, while yes, in-person meetings are preferable, they are not always viable; the bigger the group, the more help is needed through technology if there are no other means to connect. Conversely, Peter stated that "technology is gendered algorithms... We need to be aware of the power structures inherent in the technologies and in the way they operate." He stressed the importance of knowing our interest bases and being authentic about what we want to achieve, being realistic and curious about these power relations within technology.

The discussion was brought to a close by a series of thought experiments on what putting the planet first would mean for "our holy grail: creativity." Would we support each idea in creativity just because it increases our freedom of choice or other values? Should we only support those creative ideas which are good for the planet, or would this limit the future of technology, and thereby limit our creativity flow?

Peter was adamant that this line of thinking was somewhat outdated as long as inequalities continue to exist and increase on such a large scale, as this hinders problem-solving more so than anything else. Eva came in from a process and functional point of view, saying that sustainability nowadays is more complex than one entity or set of ideas dictating what we can or can't do. Rather, she concluded, it's many different engines, iterations, and developments that bring a new idea or product to fruition. Sustainability is not a competition — we need good ideas and innovation to bring us ahead in the most effective manner.

Literature

*References from Chapter 3- Spot On MozART: Visualizing Music in the Digital Age

Alexander, Bryan: Academia Next. The Futures of Higher Education. Baltimore: John Hopkins University Press 2020.

Ballhausen, Thomas: Signaturen der Erinnerung. Über die Arbeit am Archiv. Wien: Edition Atelier 2015.

Behrmann, Malte: Creative Industry Management. Kultur- und Kreativwirtschaft im digitalen Wandel: Grundlagen und Definitionen. Berlin: Springer 2021.

Belliger, Andréa & Krieger, David J.: Organizing Networks. An Actor-Network Theory of Organizations. Bielefeld: transcript 2016.

Biggs, Michael & Karlsson, Henrik (Ed.): The Routledge Companion to Research in the Arts. London: Routledge 2012.

Creswell, John W.: Research Design. Qualitative, Quantitative, and Mixed Methods Approaches. London: Sage 2014.

de Souza, Allan: How Art Can Be Thought. A Handbook for Change. Durham: Duke University Press 2018.

Hauschildt, Jürgen & Salomo, Sören: Innovationsmanagement. 5. Überarbeitete, ergänzte und aktualisierte Auflage. München: Verlag Franz Vahlen 2011.

Jain, Ravi K. et al.: Managing Research, Development, and Innovation. Hoboken, Nj: Wiley 2010.

Jackson, Alecia Y. & Mazzei, Lisa A.: Thinking with Theory in Qualitative Research. Viewing Data Across Multiple Perspectives. London: Routledge 2012.

Laloux, Frederic: Reinventing Organizations. Ein Leitfaden zur Gestaltung sinnstiftender Formen der Zusammenarbeit. München: Verlag Franz Vahlen 2015.

Leavy, Patricia: Method Meets Art. Art-Based Research Practice. New York: The Guilford Press 2020.

Monk, Ian & Levin Becker, Daniel (Ed.): All That Is Evident Is Suspect. Readings from the Oulipo 1963-2018. San Francisco: McSweeney's 2018.

Nelson, Maggie: On Freedom. Four Songs of Care and Constraint. London: Jonathan Cape 2021.

Pigrum, Derek: Teaching Creativity. Multi-mode Transitional Practices. London: Continuum 2009.

Thomas, Matthew K.E. & Bellingham, Robin (Ed.): Post-Qualitative Research and Innovative Methodologies. London: Bloomsbury Academic 2020.

Valtonen, Anna & Nikkinen, Petra (Ed.): Designing Change. New Opportunities for Organisations. Espoo: Aalto University/Aalto ARTS Books 2022.

Weinreich, Uwe: Lean Digitization. Digitale Transformation durch agiles Management. Berlin: Springer

Weblinks:

https://www.spotonmozart.at
https://www.moz.ac.at

**References from Chapter 10- Decide to be creative! An exploration of the role of creative self-beliefs in translating creative potential into creative behavior

Beghetto, R. A., & Dilley, A. E. (2016). Creative aspirations or pipe dreams? Toward understanding creative mortification in children and adolescents. New Directions for Child and Adolescent Development, 151, 85–95.

Bandura, A. (1997). Self-efficacy: The exercise of control. Macmillan.

Benedek, M., Jauk, E., Sommer, M., Arendasy, M., & Neubauer, A. C. (2014). Intelligence, creativity, and cognitive control: The common and differential involvement of executive functions in intelligence and creativity. Intelligence, 46, 73–83.

Karwowski, M., & Beghetto, R. A. (2019). Creative behavior as agentic action. Psychology of Aesthetics, Creativity, and the Arts, 13(4), 402–415. https://doi.org/10.1037/aca0000190

Karwowski, M., Czerwonka, M., Lebuda, I., Jankowska, D. M., & Gajda, A. (2020). Does thinking about Einstein make people entity theorists? Examining the malleability of creative mindsets. Psychology of Aesthetics, Creativity, and the Arts, 14(3), 361–366. https://doi.org/10.1037/aca0000226

Karwowski, M., Lebuda, I., & Beghetto, R. A. (2019). Creative Self-Beliefs. In J. C. Kaufman & R. J. Sternberg (Eds.), The Cambridge Handbook of Creativity (2nd ed., pp. 396–418). Cambridge University Press. https://doi.org/10.1017/9781316979839.021

Lebuda, I., Zielińska, A., & Karwowski, M. (2021). On surface and core predictors of real-life creativity. Thinking Skills and Creativity, 42, 100973. https://doi.org/10.1016/j.tsc.2021.100973

Nusbaum, E. C., Silvia, P. J., & Beaty, R. E. (2014). Ready, set, create: What instructing people to "be creative" reveals about the meaning and mechanisms of divergent thinking. Psychology of Aesthetics, Creativity, and the Arts, 8(4), 423–432. https://doi.org/10.1037/a0036549

Sternberg, R. J. (2002). Creativity as a decision. American Psychologist, 57, 376. Sternberg, R. J. (2003). The development of creativity as a decision-making process. In Sawyer, R. Keith, V. John-Steiner, S. Moran, R. J. Sternberg, D. H. Feldman, J. Nakamura, & M. Csikszentmihalyi (Eds.), Creativity and development (pp. 91–138). Oxford University Press.

Zielińska, A., Lebuda, I., Jankowska, D. M., & Karwowski, M. (2021). Self-Regulation in Creative Learning: Agentic Perspective. Creativity. Theories – Research - Applications, 8(1), 52–71. https://doi.org/10.2478/ctra-2021-0005

***References from Chapter 12- Creativity: What We Know (And What We Don't)

Abraham, A. (2018). The Neuroscience of Creativity. Cambridge University Press.
Baas, M., De Dreu, C. K., & Nijstad, B. A. (2008). A meta-analysis of 25 years of mood-creativity research: Hedonic tone, activation, or regulatory focus?. Psychological Bulletin, 134(6), 779.

Beaty, R. E., Kenett, Y. N., Christensen, A. P., Rosenberg, M. D., Benedek, M., Chen, Q., ... & Silvia, P. J. (2018). Robust prediction of individual creative ability from brain functional connectivity. Proceedings of the National Academy of Sciences, 115(5), 1087-1092.

Beaty, R. E., & Silvia, P. J. (2012). Why do ideas get more creative across time? An executive interpretation of the serial order effect in divergent thinking tasks. Psychology of Aesthetics, Creativity, and the Arts, 6(4), 309.

Benedek, M., Karstendiek, M., Ceh, S. M., Grabner, R. H., Krammer, G., Lebuda, I., ... & Kaufman, J. C. (2021). Creativity myths: Prevalence and correlates of misconceptions on creativity. Personality and Individual Differences, 182, 111068.

Cropley, D. H., Cropley, A. J., Kaufman, J. C., & Runco, M. A. (Eds.). (2010). The Dark Side of Creativity. Cambridge university press.

Fürst, G., & Grin, F. (2021). Multicultural experience and multilingualism as predictors of creativity. International Journal of Bilingualism, 25(5), 1486-1494.

Jauk, E., Benedek, M., Dunst, B., & Neubauer, A. C. (2013). The relationship between intelligence and creativity: New support for the threshold hypothesis by means of empirical breakpoint detection. Intelligence, 41(4), 212-221.

Kaufman, S. B., Kozbelt, A., Silvia, P., Kaufman, J. C., Ramesh, S., & Feist, G. J. (2016). Who finds Bill Gates sexy? Creative mate preferences as a function of cognitive ability, personality, and creative achievement. The Journal of Creative Behavior, 50(4), 294-307.

Kenett, Y. N., & Faust, M. (2019). A semantic network cartography of the creative mind. Trends in Cognitive Sciences, 23(4), 271-274.

Merseal, H. M., Cortes, R. A., Cotter, K. N., & Beaty, R. E. (2022). Trends in translational creativity research: Introduction to the special issue. Translational Issues in Psychological Science, 8(1), 1-5. https://doi.org/10.1037/tps0000331

Norlander, T. (1999). Inebriation and inspiration? A review of the research on alcohol and creativity. The Journal of Creative Behavior, 33(1), 22-44.

Shin, S. J., Kim, T. Y., Lee, J. Y., & Bian, L. (2012). Cognitive team diversity and individual team member creativity: A cross-level interaction. Academy of Management Journal, 55(1), 197-212.

Torrance, E. P. 2008. Torrance Tests of Creative Thinking: Norms-Technical Manual, Verbal Forms A and B. Bensenville, IL: Scholastic Testing Service.

****References from Chapter 13 - Knowledge and Creativity

Kenett, Y. N., & Faust, M. (2019). A semantic network cartography of the creative mind.

Produced and published by:
BoD – Books on Demand, Norderstedt
ISBN: 9783757823504